WILLIAM PENN

CHAPTER I

WILLIAM PENN GOES TO COLLEGE

THE middle of the seventeenth century was a
very exciting time in England. The Cavaliers
of King Charles the First were fighting the Roundheads of Oliver Cromwell, and the whole country
was divided into King's men and Parliament's
men. On the side of Cromwell and the Parliament was Admiral William Penn, who had in
1646 been given command of a squadron of fighting ships with the title of Vice Admiral of Ireland,
and who had proved to be an expert navigator
and sea-fighter. He had married Margaret Jas-
per, the daughter of an English merchant who
lived in Rotterdam, and when he went to sea, he
left his wife and children in the pretty little English village of Wanstead, in the county of Essex.

The Admiral's son William was born on October
14, 1644, when four great battles of the English

Civil War had already been fought: Edge Hill,
Newbury, Nantwich, and Marston Moor. The
Roundheads were winning the victories, and these
Puritan soldiers, fired with religious zeal, and taking such striking names as "Praise God Barebones"
and "Sergeant Hew Agag in Pieces before the
Lord," were battering down castles and cathedrals,
smashing stained-glass windows and pipe organs,
and showing their hatred of nobles and of churchmen in every way they could think of. The wife
of Admiral Penn, however, lived quietly in her
country home, and by the time William was five
years old the Cavaliers had lost the battle of
Naseby, had surrendered Bridgewater and Bristol,
and King Charles the First had been beheaded.
A new England, a Puritan England, had taken the
place of the old England, but the boy was too
young to understand the difference. He knew that
his father was now fighting the Dutch, but he was
chiefly interested in the games he played with his
schoolmates at Wanstead and with the boys from
the neighboring village of Chigwell.

Now Admiral Penn had fought on the side of
the Roundheads because the English navy had
sided with the Parliament, while the English army
had largely sided with the king, and not from any
real love of Oliver Cromwell and the Puritans.

He was indeed a Royalist at heart, and had very little patience with the new religious ideas that were becoming so popular in England. The people in Wanstead, however, were mostly Puritans, and young William, boy though he was, heard so much about their religion that he became a little Puritan like his playmates. Some of the fathers and mothers boasted that they had seen "visions," and soon the children were repeating what their parents said. Strange experiences of that kind were in the air, and so little William Penn, when he was only eleven, claimed that he had himself met with such an adventure, and seen a "vision" too.

The news of this story of William's would have annoyed his father, but the Admiral was too much concerned at the time with his own difficulties to give much heed to his son. Admiral Penn had sent word secretly to the exiled son of Charles I. that he would enter his service against Oliver Cromwell, and the latter heard of it, and when the Admiral returned to England, Cromwell had him clapped into the Tower of London to keep him out of mischief. Mrs. Penn and her children went up to London and lodged in a little court near the Tower, where they might at least be near the Admiral. Presently the Admiral, stripped of his commission, was released, and left London for a country place in Ireland that Cromwell had given him for his earlier services. There he stayed until the Royalists got the better of the Roundheads, and Charles II. was placed on the English throne. Then Admiral Penn hurried to welcome the new king, was made a knight for his loyalty, and began to bask in the full sunshine of royal favor. He was now a great figure at court, was a man of wealth, and a close friend and adviser to the king's brother, James, Duke of York, Lord High Admiral of England. Being so thoroughly a Royalist and Church of England man himself, it never occurred to him that his son William was already more than half a Puritan.

The Admiral sent his son to the aristocratic Christ Church College at Oxford when William was sixteen, and entered him as a gentleman commoner, which gave him a higher social standing than most of the students. The father meant his son to be a courtier and man of fashion, and wanted him to make friends among the young aristocrats of Oxford. But Oxford University, like the rest of England, had felt the Puritan influence during the days when Cromwell was Lord Protector, and although the Cavaliers did everything they could to restore the revelries and sports of the good old

times of Charles the First, some of the soberer
notions of the Puritans still stuck to the place.
The Puritans were fond of long sermons and much
psalm-singing, and shook their heads at all games
and light entertainments. The Royalists stopped
as much psalm-singing as they could, while they
themselves got up Morris dances and May-day
games and all kinds of masques and revels. Sometimes they went too far in their desire to oppose
the Puritans, and indulged in all sorts of dissipa-
tions. Young William Penn, and many other boys
at college, thought the Royalists were too dissolute, and leaned toward the Puritan standards;
but he was the son of a knight and a courtier, as
well as being naturally fond of sports and gayety,
and so he did not dress so soberly nor attend so
many sermons as some of his college friends.
When the king's brother, Henry, Duke of Glouces-
ter, died of smallpox, Oxford University issued a
volume of verses, called "Threnodia," on the
duke's death, and young William Penn sent in some
Latin lines for the volume. In some matters he
was a strong king's man, but in others he was more
fond of the stricter Puritan notions. Withal he
was a fairly good student, a popular young fellow,
and something of an athlete. He might very
well have graduated and followed his father to the

king's court at London had not a new and strange
religious party caught his wide-awake attention
while he was at college.

When William Penn went to Oxford, some people
in England were beginning to be called Quakers,
or, as they preferred to be known, Friends. They
were almost as much opposed to the Puritans as
they were to the Royalists, who belonged to the
Church of England. They were a religious sect,
and more. They refused to pay the tithes or
taxes for the support of the Established Church,
they refused to take an oath in the law courts,
they would wear their hats in court and in the
presence of important persons. They called every
one by his first name, and would not use any
title, even that of Mister; "thee" and "thou"
took the place of " you," although those pronouns
had customarily only been used to servants.
Nothing gave so much offense to a Royalist as to
have a Quaker say "thee" or "thou" to him.
They preached in taverns and in highways, and
walked the streets uttering prophecies of doom in
a loud singsong voice. Either because of this
trembling mode of speech, or because their leader,
George Fox, had bade the magistrates tremble at
the word of the Lord, they were called Quakers.

It seemed to both the Churchmen and the

Puritans that these Quakers were breaking away from all forms of religion; they did not believe in baptism nor in the communion service; they would not listen to clergymen or hired preachers, and often they sat silent in their meetings, only speaking when one of them felt inspired to address them. Quietness was their watchword, and so they condemned all sports and games, theaters, dancing, card playing; they disapproved of soldiers and of fighting; they kept out of politics, and they dressed as soberly as possible. Their leader, George Fox, was a strange person, very brave but very excitable, and he managed to rouse discussion wherever he went. Again and again he was put in jail; he was stoned and abused and laughed at; but such was his power that more and more people came to follow him, and admired and reverenced and loved him.

It may seem strange that the Quakers should have appealed so strongly to a youth like William Penn, who was a gentleman commoner at the most aristocratic college in England, a good-looking, popular, sport-loving fellow, surrounded by the sons of noblemen and courtiers. The answer must be that he was by nature serious-minded and very much interested in questions of religion. More than that, he had in him a strong streak of heroism which made it easy for him to throw his whole soul into a cause that appealed to him. Whatever Penn was he was never lukewarm, but ardent and fiery and always tremendously in earnest.

He left Oxford after about two years, and there is a story that he was expelled because he and some friends refused to obey a college rule about the wearing of gowns and tore off the surplices that were worn by the Church of England students. He had heard the Quaker preacher Thomas Loe, and although he had not actually joined the Society of Friends he was already largely of a mind to. From college he went to his father's house in London, and then Admiral Sir William Penn found that his son was not at all the worldly-minded youth he had hoped, but a young man of quite a different sort. He did not care for the life of a cavalier or court gallant, but wanted to go to strange religious meetings. The Admiral begged and entreated, threatened and stormed, used arguments and even blows, and finally in a fit of rage drove his son from his house. But Lady Penn pleaded for her son, and the Admiral at length allowed William to return to his home.

CHAPTER II

The Early Quakers

To understand the history of William Penn we must have a clear idea of the Quaker faith in the time of Charles II. All through the Middle Ages the Christian Church, which was the Roman Catholic Church, had built up a network of beliefs that people took for granted, so that men never used their minds where religion was concerned, but were, to all intents and purposes, merely children, believing whatever the priests told them to believe. For centuries England, as well as all of Western Europe, had taken its creed directly from the Pope and his clergy, no more doubting the truth of what was told them than a child doubts the truth of the multiplication-table. But at length certain men of unusual independence of mind, men such as Martin Luther and John Calvin, became restless under the arbitrary teachings of the Pope and dared to question whether the priests were always right, no matter what they said. These men, and others like them, took part in what was

known as the Reformation, an era in which men
began to do a little thinking for themselves. The
revival of the classical learning of Greece and
Rome and the invention of the printing-press
helped this new freedom of thought greatly. The
first books to come from the printing-presses were
copies of the Bible, which had formerly been beyond
the reach of all but the priests, and as men soon
translated the Scriptures from Latin into English
and French and German and other languages, the
people gradually became able to read the Old and
New Testaments for themselves. The Bible was
no longer a sealed book, from which the clergy gave
the ordinary man and woman as much or as little
as they thought good. It was free to all, and new
teachers began to explain its meaning according to
their own ideas.

It took a long time, however, for men to break
away from the implicit obedience they had given
for centuries to the Church of Rome. The most
daring reformers only rid themselves of one or
two dogmas at a time. Wycliffe, the first great
leader of the Reformation in England, only denied
a part of the truth of the Mass, and kept almost all
the rest of the Catholic belief. Huss, who followed
him, only dared to doubt the truth of certain of
the miracles, though he did declare that he believed

in religious liberty. Martin Luther himself devoted most of his eloquence to attacking the sale
of indulgences, which had been carried to great
excess. Later he grew so bold as to oppose the
authority of the Pope, but he still held to the larger
part of the creed of the early Church.

In England Henry the Eighth had broken with
the Pope chiefly because the latter had refused to
grant him a divorce from Catherine of Aragon and
not because of any great difference in religious
views. This break, however, gave the reformers
an official position in England, and led to the
establishment of the Church of England, which
was called a Protestant Church to distinguish it
from the Catholic. Henry's daughter, Mary, was
a Catholic, and her reign saw a bitter struggle in
England between Catholics and the new reform
Protestants. Mary's sister, Elizabeth, favored the
Protestants, and with her reign the new Church
actually came into its own, and the teachings of the
Reformation began to bear fruit.

Very gradually, then, men came to think more
and more freely for themselves. The Church of
England discarded some of the beliefs of the
Roman Catholic Church, but held to a great many
of them, and once it became well fixed as the
Established Church of England it also became

conservative, and insisted that people should obey
its teachings, just as the Catholic Church had
done. But the idea of the right of every one to
think for himself had been set rolling and could not
be stopped. Men and women who wished liberty
to worship God in their own way went to America
and founded communities with that principle as
their basis, while others in England began to show
their independence of the Established Church, and
began to league themselves together as Presbyterians or Lutherans, under a number of different
names, and many were often spoken of as Puritans.
The Civil War between Charles I. and Parliament
was also largely a war between the men of the
Church of England and the Puritans. Then, when
the Puritans had won a place for themselves and a
certain amount of power, they in their turn became conservative, and wanted to impose their
own beliefs and religious observances upon the
rest of England.

By this time, however, men had grown so used
to freedom of thought in religious matters that
every little group had its own peculiar creed. Any
man of an original turn of mind could start a new
sect and win converts. The Puritans themselves
were not sufficiently liberal to suit men who now
took pride in recognizing no authority in questions

as to what they should think. Most of these small sects played very small parts in history. Some, such as the Independents, the Anabaptists, and the Pietists, flourished for a short time, and then became merged in other sects. The Quakers, however, made a much stronger appeal than many of the others, and drew into their ranks a great number of those who were dissatisfied with the conservatism of the Catholics, the Church of England, and the Puritans.

The reason the Quakers absorbed many of the other sects and grew so rapidly, and doubtless the chief reason why they appealed so strongly to the liberal mind of young William Penn, was that they set forth as their aim the definite plan of returning to primitive Christianity in its simplest form. To those men and women who thought that all religion had become hopelessly corrupt through the ignorance and fraud and cruelty of the priesthood that had so long controlled the church, the Quaker leaders tried to show that original Christianity was as pure and simple as ever. What they wanted was that people should return to the doctrines of the Christian Church as they were before the Bishop of Rome became Pope, and before the priests interpreted the Bible as best suited themselves. The Quaker teachers declared that the Church of

England and the Puritans had gone only half-
way; they were still making their appeal chiefly
to the rich and influential; this new religion was to
satisfy the ordinary, the poor, the simple, those
who cared little for wealth or high station. No
wonder that this direct appeal made many converts
among the great mass of English people, who were
tired of the endless struggles between kings and
parliaments, bishops and ministers.

In their desire to return to the simplicity of the
early days of the Christian Church, the Quakers
became earnest students of those who were called
the fathers of the Church, — the early writers on
Christianity, such as Tertullian, Justin Martyr,
Irenæus, Cyprian, and Origen. There they found
the principles of a religious worship that was free
from all elaborate ceremonies. There they found
an absolute freedom of opinion; preachers who
served without pay and solely because they felt
spiritually called upon to preach; they also found
that many of the early Christians were opposed
to war and to the taking of oaths, and that they
protested against the use of titles, elaborate
clothes, and entertainments that tended to corrupt the tastes. Therefore it was easy for the
Quaker leaders to show their audiences that the
ideas they were urging upon them were actually

the beliefs of the earliest Christians, and were therefore worthy of earnest consideration.

Other people had urged a return to primitive Christianity earlier than the Quakers. The Albigenses, in the south of France during the thirteenth century, and the Waldenses, who lived in the valleys of Piedmont, in Northern Italy, both held somewhat similar ideas, but in each case the iron hand of persecution had suppressed them. The Quakers would doubtless have met with a similar fate had they come into existence a century earlier, for they held even more extreme views than had the Albigenses. But by the reign of Charles II. the principles of the Reformation had made such headway that it was impossible to do away with a new form of religion by killing its converts. The government was willing to go a certain distance in suppressing these new heretics, and ordinances were passed empowering justices to imprison any who denied the validity of the sacraments of baptism and the Lord's Supper. Quakers who held meetings in the streets or market-places were liable to be arrested for committing a breach of the peace, and their missionaries were often treated as vagrants and whipped; but these were extremely light punishments compared with those that had been inflicted earlier.

Although there were a few men and women among the early Quakers who made themselves conspicuous by their extreme views, as there are among the people of any sect, the Quakers were for the greater part a remarkably sober, sensible, and law-abiding party. The Catholics, the Puritans, the Presbyterians, and others had never hesitated to hold their meetings in secret when the laws seemed too severe against them. The Quakers, however, never held secret meetings; they performed their duties openly, no matter how much the magistrates were opposed to them. They argued their cause freely and openly on all occasions, and they wrote a great many pamphlets setting forth their belief and also telling to what persecutions they had been subjected. These tracts were widely distributed, and served to call attention to the reasonableness of their cause and to win sympathy for their struggles with the law.

They also soon showed the English virtue of obstinacy in their cause; for no matter how many times they were imprisoned or arrested they continued steadfastly on their course. At first people laughed at the Quakers' custom of holding their religious meetings in prison just as they might have held them in their meetinghouses, but before long the laughter changed to respect, and finally became sincere admiration. The Puritans, who had themselves had to endure the same sort of treatment a little while before, could appreciate the attitude of this still younger religious movement, and though they did not sympathize with the views of the Quakers they came to admire their courageous independence.

William Penn, young as he was, saw that the Quakers stood at the opposite pole from what he had come to consider a superstitious priesthood; he saw that with them religion had nothing to do with politics or power; that it was destined to stand for a more reasonable and simple faith than any of the others then existing in England. It was the latest form of that great wave of liberty that had begun with the Reformation; and as the latest it appealed to him as the most liberal form. He had a natural interest in religion, a natural earnestness of mind that led him to study the new movement, and sufficient strength of judgment to be able to find the truth in it that was hidden from many others. Add to this a basis of heroism, inherited from adventure-loving ancestors, and it is not difficult to see how the young man was led to sympathize with, and then to adopt, the Quaker faith as his own.

c

CHAPTER III

WILLIAM PENN TRAVELS

WHEN his son William came home from Oxford, Admiral Penn was a prominent figure in London. He held numerous offices, for he was a Naval Commissioner, a Member of Parliament, Governor of Kinsale, Admiral of Ireland, a Member of the Council of Munster, and a favorite of King Charles and the Duke of York. He was in high hopes that he would soon be made a peer. His wife, Lady Penn, and his daughter Margaret, or Peg, as she was usually called, were fond of society and fashion. It was somewhat natural, therefore, that Admiral Penn should not altogether understand or appreciate the new religious views of his son William. He thought the youth exceedingly willful, but could not believe that his interest in the new movement was anything more than a passing whim. Therefore, in order to interest William in other things, he introduced him to his own friends and showed him something of the pleasant side of life at King Charles's court. He took William to suppers at the Bear Inn, and to plays at Drury Lane Theater. There was a satire on the Puritans, called "The Jovial Crew," then being given at a theater known as "The Cockpit," and the Admiral took William there in order to show him how absurd Puritans, and all the newer religious sects, actually were. But no matter how heartily the Admiral laughed and encouraged his son to laugh, he could not get William to throw himself into the pleasures of London life as readily as he thought a normal young fellow ought to.

The father was really very fond of his son, and spe t considerable time in casting about as to what was best for his boy. At length it occurred to him that a visit to the gay city of Paris would entertain William, and drive out of his head some of his strange Oxford notions. Some of his college friends were going to France to study, and the Admiral arranged that William should go abroad with them. Some of them were of high rank, and they would easily have entrance to the best French society.

The young men were made welcome in Paris. Penn was presented to the king, Louis XIV, and was charmed by the brilliance of the French court. He made the acquaintance of entertaining people, and he had at least one adven-

ture. The story is told that as he was returning late one night from a ball, he was stopped
by a rogue who angrily called out to him to draw
his sword and defend himself. The rascal flashed
his own rapier before Penn's eyes, and declared
that Penn had insulted him, — that he had bowed
and taken off his hat politely to the young Englishman, but that the latter had paid no attention to
him. Penn answered courteously that he had not
seen the stranger, and so could not have insulted
him by failing to bow to him. The stranger,
however, only grew more excited, and insisted that
Penn must fight him or he would run him through.

Penn saw that argument was useless, and being
by that time angry himself, drew his own sword
and stood on defense. The street was dark, but
a small crowd had gathered, attracted by the loud
words, and several men announced that they would
see fair play. The swords flashed in a few passes,
and then Penn showed himself the more skillful
swordsman. With a twist of his rapier he sent his
opponent's sword flying into the air. The crowd
expected him to attack his opponent again, but
instead Penn stooped, and, picking up the other
man's sword, handed it back to him with a bow,
saying that he hoped the Frenchman was satisfied.
News of the little encounter quickly spread among

the young Englishman's friends, and on the strength of it he became quite a hero.

Meantime the Admiral in London was much pleased with the reports he had of William's success in the social world of Paris. He wanted him to have a more thorough education, however, than Oxford afforded, and so made arrangements that he should go to Professor Moses Amyrault, at Saumur, to live in his home and study under him. Penn followed his father's wishes and spent some time at Saumur, becoming well acquainted with the language and literature of France, and having a pleasant time generally. Afterwards with a friend he traveled through Switzerland into Italy, making a part of the "grand tour" that in those days was considered an important part of the education of every young Englishman of fashion.

When he returned to London, he was very French and very gallant; indeed, he was so much a gentleman of fashion that Admiral Penn was really delighted. He had hopes, now, that William would, after all, follow in his own footsteps, and become a figure at the king's court. With that end in view Sir William entered his son at Lincoln's Inn to study law. If he was to hold important offices in the government of his country, he must have some knowledge of law; and, besides, the legal training

would bring him into contact with rising men of
good families. So William began his studies, and
the Admiral, well pleased, embarked with the
Duke of York to fight the Dutch.

Penn's studies at Lincoln's Inn were interrupted
by the great plague that swept over London and
devastated the city. Like most other people of
means he left the place and went into the country,
carrying with him memories of the sick and suffering in the wretched, ill-kept streets and alleys. He
was lonely in the country, and he could not help
remembering the scenes in the plague-stricken
town; so that when his father came back and
joined him, the Admiral found William again in
his former speculative frame of mind. To once
more divert his mind, Sir William sent him to enter
the service of the Duke of Ormond, who, as Lord
Lieutenant of Ireland, held quite a court in the
city of Dublin.

The Admiral was Governor of Kinsale, in County
Cork, and William was given charge of his father's
affairs there, as well as being employed in various
ways by the Duke of Ormond. He enjoyed this
work, and when there was a mutiny of the soldiers
at Carrickfergus, he took a large part in quelling it,
so pleasing the duke by his ability that the latter
suggested that young Penn should be made cap-

tain of the Admiral's troop of soldiers. Sir William was glad to hear such good reports of his son, but did not think him fitted as yet to command his soldiers.

Young Penn was enjoying life on his father's estate and at the duke's court in Dublin, and was decidedly the courtier and man of affairs; when one day, being in Cork on business, he happened to hear the preaching of Thomas Loe, a man he had already heard at Oxford. The message of that sermon lay in the words, "There is a faith which overcomes the world, and there is a faith which is overcome by the world." It made a deep impression on the young man. Was his faith of the type that overcomes the world? Or was it of the kind that is overcome by pride of place and fortune? He feared that thus far his faith had shown itself of the latter sort. He gave a great deal of thought to that message of Thomas Loe.

Being so ardent by nature, he determined that his faith should overcome the temptations that surrounded him. He would fight by the side of those who believed in the simple teachings of early Christianity and who were unhampered by the forms and ceremonies the other churches had imposed upon their members. Thomas Loe's sermon was the spark that set Penn's zeal ablaze. He made up his mind to become a Quaker, in spite of all that his family or friends might say. The new faith had made its appeal to the deepest springs of his earnest and religious nature.

So William Penn, already considerable of a courtier, became a Quaker; and contrived, strange though it seems, to be both things at one and the same time. His father had been both a Roundhead and a Royalist, though in his case it had always been from motives of self-interest. The son was now to combine two widely different types of man, but with him this resulted entirely from the two sides of his nature. Yet it was a very odd combination, that of a Quaker and a courtier, and one sure to bring him into many curious situations.

CHAPTER IV

THE YOUNG QUAKER COURTIER

WILLIAM PENN had studied at Oxford, had
traveled and mixed with gay people on the Continent, had been entered as a law student at Lincoln's Inn, had been employed by the Duke of
Ormond in Ireland, and now had decided to throw
in his lot with the people of this new religion that
had suddenly sprung up in England and who called
themselves by the simple name of Friends. He
stayed in Ireland, looking after his father's business
at Kinsale, still wearing the bright clothes of a
cavalier, but he went regularly to all the meetings
of Quakers that were held in Cork. These meetings were no more popular with the government in
Ireland than in England, and while Penn was
attending one on September 3, 1667, several
constables, with a squad of soldiers, appeared at
the doors and arrested everybody on the charge
of holding a riotous assembly. There is a story,
perhaps not altogether true, that, as the first
soldier entered the hall to break up the meeting,

William Penn seized him by the collar, and would have thrown him down the stairs had not some older members interfered and told the young man that such an act would be inconsistent with the Quaker's love of peace.

Penn, however, was probably not as hot-headed as the story would indicate; he went with the other Quakers to the mayor, and that official, seeing that the young man wore cavalier dress, offered to set him free if he would give bond for his future good behavior. Penn would not agree to this; instead he argued that the arrest of the Quakers was altogether unlawful. Thereupon he was sent to prison, and from there he wrote a remarkably well-worded letter to the Earl of Orrery, the Lord President of Munster, setting forth the injustice of interfering in such a way with any people's religion.

The young man of three-and-twenty had stood by his new comrades, and had written an excellent letter on their behalf, but there was no gainsaying the fact that he himself was in a rather bad plight. The dashing young cavalier, son of the courtier Sir William Penn, and a member of the Duke of Ormond's court at Dublin, had actually been caught in all his fine clothes at a meeting of the Quakers, and had been marched off to prison with a troop of his new friends. That was an entertaining bit of gossip; but as soon as it came to the ears of the Earl of Orrery, that nobleman, being a friend of Admiral Penn, and anxious to rescue his son from the company of the Quakers, ordered that William should be released from prison. Time and again it happened that William Penn, being a cavalier as well as a Quaker, was gently handled by cavalier officers on account of his rank and position.

The Admiral had heard of this new "prank," as he chose to call it, of his son, and had ordered William home. William obeyed willingly enough. In his famous Diary we find Mr. Pepys, who was no great admirer of Admiral Penn, writing at this time: "At night comes Mrs. Turner to see us; and then among other talk she tells me that Mr. William Penn, who is lately come over from Ireland, is a Quaker again, or some very melancholy thing; that he cares for no company, nor comes into any; which is a pleasant thing after his being abroad so long and his father such a hypocritical rogue."

But other surprises were awaiting Admiral Penn. He soon found that William kept his hat on when talking to him, which, in the Admiral's opinion, was a mark of great disrespect. He sternly asked

William what he meant by this. William boldly
answered that it was a Quaker custom and that he
was a Quaker. The father argued, pleaded, and
stormed, and finally asked if William would not at
least take off his hat in the presence of three persons, — his father, the king, and the Duke of
York. This was a great concession on the part of
the Admiral, and shows that he must at last have
waked up to the fact of his son's determination.
But all William would answer was that he would
"consider the matter."

This answer made Sir William furious. He
thought his son meant to ask the advice of some
of his new friends. The son, however, asked no
advice, but after long thought announced that he
could not grant his father's request.

Then the Admiral, in a great huff, turned William out of the house, and the latter went to visit
various friends, his mother secretly sending him
money from time to time. Finally Lady Penn
won her husband's consent to allowing William to
return home; but his father treated William like
a stranger and gave up trying to help a son, who,
in his opinion, was such an ungrateful and stiff-
necked fellow.

The people of the court and town in the England of Charles II. were a very dissipated and

ADMIRAL SIR WILLIAM PENN, FATHER OF WILLIAM PENN.

From the portrait by Peter Van Dyke.

unprincipled set. Most of the fashionable people were proud of their lack of morals, and the plays, the writings, and even the speech of the ruling class were coarse and vulgar beyond belief. William Penn saw all this, and his nature, being on a higher plane and more serious than that of his father's friends, turned instinctively to those who were living clean and respectable lives. In the jumble of new ideas and new religions he found comfort in the simplest and quietest sect; and now, having publicly declared himself a Quaker, he asked permission to be one of their preachers.

The Quakers were glad to have a man of William Penn's education and position join their ranks, and when he was twenty-four, he was accepted as one of their regular preachers. Several other men of his own type joined the new sect at about the same time, and these men, having better judgment than the earliest leaders, began to do away with the rather extreme preachings of Fox, and taught a simple and easily understood Christianity. Penn himself kept his cavalier dress, and even continued for a time to wear his sword, which was a sign of a person of fashion. He asked the advice of George Fox about keeping his sword, and the latter, in spite of his extreme views, said, "I advise thee to wear it as long as thou canst."

The new recruit made himself very useful to the
religious party he had joined. Besides preaching,
he wrote a number of tracts, the first of which he
called "Truth Exalted." In this he attacked,
according to the custom of the times, all religious
views that differed from his own, and answered
the criticisms of other sects. He was even more
useful in interceding for Quakers who had been
put in prison. Having friends at court, and being
still regarded as something of a courtier, he could
appeal to the officers of state better than others of
the new sect. His arguments in favor of setting
the Quaker prisoners at liberty were listened to
respectfully by the high officials, but. his requests
at that time were not granted.

The young preacher and tract writer soon had
his hands full with heated arguments and stormy
disputes. He wrote a pamphlet called "The
Guide Mistaken," and at about the same time two
men who belonged to the congregation of the
Presbyterian preacher Thomas Vincent in London
became Quakers. Thomas Vincent was very angry
and called Penn unpleasant names. Thereupon
Penn and his friend George Whitehead challenged
Vincent to an open debate in the latter's church.
The challenge was accepted.

Penn and Whitehead went to Vincent's church,

which was crowded, and as they pushed their way forward Vincent denounced them in no measured words. The two Quakers joined in the wordy warfare, and began a heated religious argument, while the congregation hissed and flung at them such names as "blasphemers" and "villains." Vincent himself kept interrupting, and at length, pretending to be shocked at what the two men were saying, began to pray for them. The people blew out the candles that lighted the church and tried to eject the two Quakers. The meeting ended in uproar, as was usually the case in the religious debates of those days.

Not in the least daunted by the harsh and unkind criticisms that were showered on him from all sides, Penn wrote more pamphlets, criticizing the religious views of some of the older sects, and calling many of their ideas relics of the ignorance and superstition of the Middle Ages. He was a clear and powerful writer and showed his satisfaction in stating in black and white the views that had led him to believe that truth was to be found in the religion of the Quakers rather than in any other creed. This was doubtless more satisfactory to him than holding noisy and hot-tempered arguments with opponents on street corners or in public halls, and won for him the reputation of being the

ablest of all the early Quaker leaders. Samuel
Pepys, of the famous Diary, says thus frankly of
Penn's pamphlet, "The Sandy Foundation
Shaken," "I find it so well writ as I think it is too
good for him ever to have writ it; and it is a serious
sort of book and not fit for everybody to read."
Pepys is nothing if not outspoken, and his view
was doubtless the same as that held by many fashionable people who knew the twenty-four-year-old
author and considered him a strange, misguided
young man.

Although Penn might have been allowed to
preach as he pleased in the fields or market-places,
it became quite another matter when he printed
his views and scattered them broadcast throughout
England. The Bishop of London read one of
William Penn's pamphlets and decided that the
writer was denying the fact of the divinity of Christ.
That had been made a crime by act of the English
Parliament. The young man was arrested and
imprisoned in the Tower of London, and though
his cavalier friends tried to get him out they met
with no success, and for some time they were not
allowed even to see him. Some one told him that
the Bishop of London had determined that he must
either publicly recant his impious views or spend
the rest of his life in the prison of the Tower.

Penn calmly and boldly wrote: "All is well: I wish they had told me so before, since the expecting of a release put a stop to some business; thou mayst tell my father, who I know will ask thee, these words: that my prison shall be my grave, before I will budge a jot; for I owe my conscience to no mortal man; I have no need to fear; God will make amends for all; they are mistaken in me; I value not their threats and resolutions, for they shall know I can weary out their malice and peevishness, and in me shall they all behold a resolution above fear; conscience above cruelty, and a baffle put to all their designs by the spirit of patience. . . . Neither great nor good things are ever attained without loss and hardships. He that would reap and not labor, must faint with the wind and perish in disappointments; but an hair of my head shall not fall without the Providence of my Father that is over all." Brave words these to be written by a youth in a cell of the Tower of London with small prospect of leaving it!

In his gloomy prison William Penn, like Cervantes and Walter Raleigh and John Bunyan, took to writing a book, one that he called "No Cross, No Crown." It became the most famous of all his writings. To people who read it now, when every one may think as he pleases on reli-

D

gious matters, the ideas in this book are not particularly new or striking; but Penn's statement that the cross was not meant to be considered as an outward thing of wood and nails, but as an inward inspiration, and that religion was the feeling of each individual regarding divine subjects rather than a matter of words and customs, — all this was startling and even revolutionary in that far-away time.

Fresh abuse was heaped upon him for his new writings, and he was called all the bitter names that the enemies of the Quakers could invent. Meantime he sent a letter to Lord Arlington, the Secretary of State, in which he asked to be freed from prison because he had had no trial and had not been allowed to make any defense. "Force," he wisely said, "may make hypocrites, but it can never make converts." He ended his letter boldly. "I make no apology for my letter, as a trouble — the usual style of supplicants; because I think the honor that will accrue to thee by being just and releasing the opprest exceeds the advantage that can succeed to me."

The Bishop and the government did not intend to give William Penn a chance to make a dramatic speech in defense of the Quakers at a trial, but instead they sent his father and other friends to argue with him. Their arguments had little effect, and the prisoner resigned himself to doing without a trial. He did not, however, want the world to think that he had meant to deny the divinity of Christ, and so he now wrote another pamphlet to explain his belief.

This pamphlet gave his friends a better chance to work for his release. Admiral Penn was a great friend of the king's brother, and the latter finally went to the king and persuaded him to order that William be set at liberty. So after nine months of imprisonment in the Tower the young Quaker Cavalier was free again, thanks not so much to the justice of his appeal for liberty as to his powerful friends at court.

He then began to look about to see how he could be of most service to the people who were of his own religious faith.

CHAPTER V

PENN HELPS HIS FRIENDS

By this time no one could doubt that William Penn had courage, for it took considerable bravery to face and endure imprisonment in the Tower of London as he had done, and this show of courage won admiration even from his father the Admiral. At this time Sir William was having troubles of his own. The command of his fleet had been taken from him, and he was suffering from the gout; altogether he was not in a very pleasant frame of mind, but he softened sufficiently toward his son to ask him to go again to Ireland to look after the family property there, although the request was made through William's devoted mother, and not directly. When he wrote to his son, he showed that he still rather doubted William's filial regard, for he said, "If you are ordained to be another cross to me, God's will be done, and I shall arm myself as best I can against it."

When William reached Ireland, he found the lot of the Quakers was then no better than it had been before. Their very virtues — for they were generally a hard-working and thrifty people — had set many against them. Indeed, nearly all the Quakers in Cork had been lodged in prison. Even in prison, however, they managed to carry on their affairs; for, said Penn, they turned the jail into "a meetinghouse and a workhouse, for they would not be idle anywhere."

He at once set to work to help these friends of his, and drew up a statement of the charges against the imprisoned Quakers and a defense of them, and with the help of some friends took the matter to the Lord Lieutenant at Dublin, with the result that before long the Quakers in Cork were given their freedom. Encouraged by this success, he made it his business to try to free people of his religion whenever he found them in the grasp of the law.

He managed the family estate in Ireland so well that when he went back to London in 1670, his father decided to forgive his son all the trouble he had put him to, and the courtier father and the Quaker son were completely reconciled. That did not mean, however, that the son had given up any of his opinions. It happened that at about the same time the government decided that the new religion was winning too many converts, and so put into effect a law that made unlawful any meetings for religious worship other than those held by the Church of England, by the terms of which law the magistrates were allowed to fine and imprison offenders without giving them a trial by jury; it also allowed to those who gave information about such illegal meetings one third of all the fines that were imposed. Whenever the Quakers held a meeting, therefore, some enemy was sure to give notice of it, and many Friends were imprisoned and more were fined, of course to the advantage of meddling busybodies.

One day in August William went to a Quaker meetinghouse in Gracechurch Street in London, and happened to find soldiers on guard before the building. That roused the young man's spirit, and he with some of his companions decided to hold a "silent meeting" on the sidewalk before the front doors. Presently Penn felt called upon to speak, but no sooner did he open his mouth than the soldiers pounced upon him and marched him off to the mayor.

According to Quaker custom, Penn kept his hat on before the mayor, and this so maddened that official, that he said the prisoner "should have his hat pulled off, for all he was Admiral Penn's son." Then he went on to abuse the Admiral himself, saying that he had starved the sailors of his fleet, and repeating other stories that were popular among the Admiral's enemies. He threatened to send young William to Bridewell Prison, and see that he was soundly whipped! Finally Penn was taken to a certain jail known as the Black Dog, where he was locked up with a number of other Quakers and Baptists and Independents, who had all been holding meetings in despite of the law. From the Black Dog William wrote to his father. "I am very well," said he, "and have no trouble upon my spirits, besides my absence from thee, especially at this juncture, but otherwise I can say, I was never better; and what they have to charge me with is harmless."

Penn and a man named William Mead were put on trial in the Old Bailey early in September, 1670, charged with having preached at an unlawful meeting, thereby causing a great concourse and tumult, to the disturbance of the king's peace and the great terror of many of his subjects. The two prisoners went into court with their hats on, but the officers promptly pulled the hats off. Thereupon the judges ordered the officers to put the hats again on the prisoners' heads, and began to question them about their wearing hats in court. This was regarded as very disrespectful, and could not pass unreproved. Finally the judges fined each man forty marks for such "contempt of court."

The prisoners were not allowed lawyers to defend them, and the judges proceeded to make sport of the two Quakers, as if the trial were a form of bull-baiting. Penn said that he had broken no law, but had only been worshiping God according to his own conscience. He stood up for his rights as an Englishman, and evidently impressed the jury with the justice of his claims, for, in spite of all the efforts of the judges, the jury would only find him "guilty of speaking" in Gracechurch Street, and of no crime whatever. The judges sent the jury out again and again, finally keeping them locked up for two days and nights without beds or food, but the jury were not to be browbeaten. The judges at last had to accept the verdict, "not guilty," but in revenge fined each of the prisoners forty marks and ordered them imprisoned until the fines were paid, and in addition actually fined the jury for bringing in what they considered a mock verdict!

Penn and Mead and the jury were then sent to Newgate, where they simply refused to buy their liberty by paying the unjust fines. From there Penn wrote to his father: "I intreat thee not to purchase my liberty. They will repent them of their proceedings. I am now a prisoner notoriously against law." In another letter he wrote: "Considering I cannot be free, but upon such terms as strengthening their arbitrary and base proceedings, I shall rather choose to suffer any hardship. . . . My present restraint is so far from being humor, that I would rather perish than release myself by so indirect a course as to satiate their revengeful, avaricious appetites."

The question of the right of the judges to fine the jury was finally brought before the Court of Common Pleas, which decided that the fines were unlawful, and ordered the jury set at liberty. Penn and Mead, however, had been fined for wearing their hats in court, and there is no knowing how long they might have been kept in prison if the Admiral, who was ill, had not disregarded his son's letters, and paid the fines of both Penn and Mead, when they were at once set at liberty.

Admiral Penn was very ill, and when his son returned this time from prison, he was so much concerned for the future of a young man who seemed to have such a knack for getting into trouble that he sent a friend to the Duke of York asking that the duke look after William and try to defend him before King Charles should William continue in his course of resistance to the laws. Both the duke and the king sent back their promises of help to the sick Admiral, and both of them kept those promises when William Penn needed friends later on.

As his gout increased the Admiral began to think that perhaps his son William had been right after all, and that the court of King Charles II. was not altogether what it should be. He began to talk almost like a Puritan, and to condemn many of the nobles, once his boon companions, for their loose way of living. Father and son were drawn close together in those last days of the Admiral's illness. Sir William said to his son, "Three things I commend to you:

" First. — Let nothing in this world tempt you to wrong your conscience; so you will keep peace at home, which will be a feast to you in the day of trouble.

" Secondly. — Whatever you design to do, lay it justly and time it seasonably, for that gives security and despatch.

" Lastly. — Be not troubled at disappointments, for if they may be recovered, do it; if they cannot, trouble is vain. If you could not have helped it, be content; there is often peace and profit in submitting to Providence: for afflictions make wise. If you could have helped it, let not your trouble exceed instruction for another time.

" These rules will carry you with firmness and comfort through this inconstant world."

The Admiral died on September 16, 1670, leaving William to look after his mother and his younger brother Richard. His sister Margaret had married Antony Lowther, of Maske, in Yorkshire.

PENN'S CREST.

CHAPTER VI

PENN BECOMES A MAN OF WEALTH

ADMIRAL PENN had managed to accumulate a very considerable fortune, and as a result William, the eldest son, became a rich man. His family was a prominent one, he had many influential friends, and now had plenty of money; so it was thought that he would naturally become a cavalier and gentleman of fashion. He soon made it clear, however, that he meant to retain the simple way of living adopted by the Quakers. Friends of his own age made fun of him, saying it was preposterous that a man of his means and abilities should spend his time with such dull people as those of the new religion. Sir John Robinson, the Lieutenant of the Tower of London, said to him, "I vow, Mr. Penn, I am sorry for you; you are an ingenious gentleman, all the world must allow you and do allow you that, and you have a plentiful estate. Why should you render yourself unhappy by associating with such a simple people?"

"I confess," frankly answered Penn, "I have

44

made it my choice to relinquish the company of those that are ingeniously wicked, to converse with those that are more honestly simple."

In those days men challenged each other to arguments over their religions much as they might have challenged each other to a duel. Penn enjoyed defending the Quaker cause in public. A Baptist preacher by the name of Ives denounced Penn and the Quakers in a sermon, and Penn sent him a challenge to argue the question in public.

Ives did not appear at the meeting, but his brother took his place, and, according to the rules of such arguments, had to speak first. When he had finished his argument, he, with some friends, left the hall, hoping to draw so many people away with him that few would be left to listen to his opponent. But the audience stayed to hear Penn, and he spoke so eloquently that he won the house over to his side, and cost Ives the support of many of his followers. The young Quaker was proving as convincing a speaker as he had already shown himself to be a vigorous writer. He was fast becoming a power in the new sect.

He soon found a bigger man than Ives to argue with, for as he traveled through Oxfordshire preaching the Quaker cause he came to the University

of Oxford, where he had been a student, and learned
that the young men there who were interested in
Quakerism were treated worse than ever. The
Vice Chancellor of Oxford thought that the Quakers
might become a dangerous political party, and was
doing all in his power to abolish the new religion.
Penn wrote him a letter in which, with fiery ardor,
he denounced the Vice Chancellor for his persecution of Quaker students, and followed it up with
other broadsides of attack on all who held similar
views. He was a militant character, and when he
argued before a public meeting, or wrote a letter
that was to be read by his opponents, he never
hesitated to express himself as strongly as he knew
how. So in his letter to the Vice Chancellor he
gave himself free rein. He wrote: "Shall the mul-
tiplied oppressions which thou continuest to heap
upon innocent English people for their peaceable
religious meetings pass unregarded by the Eternal
God? Dost thou think to escape his fierce wrath
and dreadful vengeance for thy ungodly and illegal
persecution of his poor children? I tell thee, no.
Better were it for thee hadst thou never been born.
Poor mushroom, wilt thou war against the Lord,
and lift up thyself in battle against the Almighty?
Canst thou frustrate his holy purposes, and bring
his determination to nought? He has decreed to

exalt himself by us, and to propagate his gospel
to the ends of the earth." Fine, spirited words
are these, worthy of the valiant courage of young
William Penn !

Penn returned from Oxfordshire to London, and
went one day to a meeting in Wheeler Street. He
started to address the meeting, but no sooner had
he begun than a sergeant marched in with a file of
soldiers, dragged him from the platform, and carried him off to the Tower. That evening an officer
and some musketeers marched him from the
Tower to Sir John Robinson, the lieutenant, who
asked him many questions, trying to make it appear that Penn was a dangerous man, who, unless
he were checked, might turn out to be another
Cromwell. Sir John, knowing that the Quakers
were opposed to all oaths, called on Penn to swear
that he would never take up arms against the king,
and also to take a solemn oath that he would never
try to make any change of government either in
church or state. This oath Penn refused to take,
saying that the Quakers were opposed to all fighting
as well as oath-taking. "If I cannot fight against
any man (much less against the king)," said he,
"what need I to take an oath not to do it? Should
I swear not to do what is already against my conscience to do?"

Sir John and the other judges sneered at him, told him that he was bringing an honorable name to disgrace, and treated his principles with haughty contempt. Finally Sir John said, "But you do nothing but stir up the people to sedition; and one of your friends told me that you preached sedition and meddled with the government."

Penn looked these accusers squarely in the face. "We have the unhappiness to be misrepresented," he answered, "and I am not the least concerned therein. Bring me the man that will dare to justify this accusation to my face, and if I am not able to make it appear that it is both my practice and all my friends' to instill principles of peace and moderation (and only war against spiritual wickedness, that all men may be brought to fear God and work righteousness), I shall contentedly undergo the severest punishment all your laws can expose me to.

"As for the king, I make this offer, that if any living can make it appear, directly or indirectly, from the time I have been called a Quaker (since from thence you date me seditious), I have contrived or acted anything injurious to his person, or the English government, I shall submit my person to your utmost cruelties, and esteem them all but a due recompense. It is hard that I, being innocent, should be reputed guilty; but the will of God be done.   I accept of bad reports as well as good."

But he could not make Sir John and the other judges believe in his innocence.   "You will be the heading of parties and drawing people after you," said Sir John, doggedly, and ordered Penn taken to Newgate, the worst prison in London, where Quakers were herded with criminals of the lowest types.

People with money could hire rooms for themselves at Newgate and so avoid some of the discomforts of that vile place, and Penn spoke to his jailers about having a private room, but they answered him so abusively and insultingly and charged him so much for a private room that he said he preferred to share the lot of the poorest criminals. And there this man of wealth and education bravely stayed for six months, writing a number of essays and a spirited religious pamphlet.   When the authorities thought the incorrigible young man must surely have learned his lesson in the wretched prison, they set him free again.   He had spent half of the last three years in jails.

When he was at length liberated, he went abroad for a time, traveling in Holland and Germany, perhaps because his stay in Newgate had injured his health, perhaps to give the suspicions concern-

E

ing him a chance to disappear. Yet, even on these journeys, whenever Penn found people showing any interest in the Quaker faith, he stopped and explained it fully to them. But in most places the new sect was looked upon as something very strange, and its members were suspected of designs against the government, so very few were anxious to learn about it.

In the autumn of 1671 Penn returned to England, and, for the first time in a number of years, lived a quiet life, giving over preaching and arguing and writing fiery pamphlets. He was twenty-seven years old, and he had fallen in love with a Quaker girl named Gulielma Maria Springett, or, as she was called by her friends, Guli Springett. Penn now busied himself in looking about for a suitable home in which to start housekeeping.

The father of William Penn's sweetheart was a young Puritan officer, who had been killed when only twenty-three years old at the siege of Bamber. Guli was born a few weeks later. Her mother, like many other people at that time, was neither satisfied with the religion of the Church of England nor that of the Puritans. Some time after her husband's death she married Isaac Pennington, and both became Quakers. So Guli was brought up in the new religion. They all lived quietly in

Buckinghamshire until his neighbors began to complain to the authorities that Isaac Pennington was "talking Quaker doctrines." Then he was put in prison, and his wife and Guli wandered from one place to another.

Guli had a considerable fortune, and her charms brought her many suitors, even though her stepfather had fallen under the displeasure of the government. But she preferred the young and ardent Quaker who had himself suffered imprisonment so often in the same good cause; and in the spring of 1672 Guli and William were married. They made their home in the country, at Rickmansworth in Hertfordshire. They were comfortably well-to-do, and as the marriage was a very happy one, it might have been predicted that William Penn would become a prosperous country squire and have done with all religious discussions that were so likely to lead to a cell in the Tower of London.

At about the same time the king, Charles II., issued a proclamation, which was known as the Declaration of Indulgence, by the terms of which he did away with all the laws against the Quakers, Presbyterians, Baptists, Roman Catholics, and all who dissented from the Church of England. There was only one objection to this decree, and that was that the king issued it by his own act, and without the approval of Parliament, which meant that Charles II. had it in mind to try to rule without Parliament if it could be managed. The Declaration of Indulgence released over four hundred Quakers from prison, and in view of that benefit Penn and others were willing to overlook for the time the king's attempt to rule solely by his own will.

From his home in the country Penn began to make short trips through Kent and Sussex and Surrey, preaching the Quaker doctrines, a free lance who served without pay and purely because he loved the work. Occasionally he took his wife with him on his travels. They went together to Bristol to welcome the Quaker leader George Fox on his return from America, and hear from him what progress the new faith was making in the strange new country across the Atlantic Ocean.

By this time the Quakers had gained so many converts that the other sects were beginning to be afraid of them, and continually challenged them to more and more of those strange public debates in which the speakers did not hesitate to call their opponents harsh names. It was said of Penn that "he never turned his back in the day of battle," and he apparently threw himself into these arguments with the same ardor his ancestors had shown in warfare. Besides taking up the cudgel in defense of the new creed, he wrote many pamphlets and letters to people who disapproved of the Quakers. In this way he kept himself very busy during the two years he lived at his charming country home.

Charles II.'s Declaration of Indulgence proved so unpopular with the Parliament that the king had soon to withdraw it, and then the old opposition to all rivals of the Church of England broke out more violently than ever. George Fox was arrested and kept in prison for a year. The king offered to give him a pardon, but the Quakers were unwilling to accept pardons, as that would imply that they had really done something that was wrong. But Fox was ill, and Penn and some others went to court and tried to secure the favor of the Duke of York in behalf of Fox. The duke was very friendly to Penn, as he had been to Penn's father, but he did nothing to free Fox. However, the Quakers soon afterward secured the release of their leader by an appeal to the law courts.

Then a man named Richard Baxter happened to go to Rickmansworth and found the place "abounding with Quakers," as he put it, "because Mr. W. Penn, their captain, dwelleth there." Baxter wanted to redeem these people from their errors and challenged Penn to an argument. They debated from ten in the morning until five in the afternoon, before a great crowd, and at the end of that time all present held to their original views, although each debater claimed the victory. Penn enjoyed this argument immensely, for he told Baxter he would like to give him a room in his house, so "that I could visit and get discourse with thee in much tender love." But Baxter did not accept that invitation, and soon afterward Mrs. Penn inherited a house and estate at Worminghurst, in Sussex, so she and her husband moved their home to that place. A little later Penn, with George Fox and other Quakers, set out on a missionary visit to Holland and Germany.

CHAPTER VII

PENN IN POLITICS

PEOPLE in Holland and Germany, as well as in England, had now felt the new spirit of religious liberty, so that William Penn and George Fox found more men and women in those countries eager to listen to their teachings than they had found elsewhere. The Quaker leaders traveled from one town to another, meeting many people, giving them copies of the pamphlets that Penn and others had written, and urging them to join the new Society of Friends. The Quaker missionaries met with considerable success, although by no means all the people who listened to them became Quakers, but many joined one or another of the new sects that were springing up at the time.

When he returned to England, Penn found the condition of the Quakers there as unsatisfactory as ever. The majority of the English people were so afraid that King Charles II. wanted to turn the country over to the Catholics that they were making the laws more and more strict against all who

were not members of the Church of England, and
this, of course, included the Quakers. They were
being fined and imprisoned right and left, and
treated worse than if they had no religion at all.

As it was against the Quaker rule to take an oath
of any kind, members of the new sect were at a great
disadvantage in courts of law and in all places
where an oath of allegiance to the government was
required. To help them in this difficulty, Penn
succeeded in inducing the House of Commons to
allow Quakers to affirm instead of taking an oath,
but before he could succeed in having the House
of Lords pass the same bill the king dissolved
Parliament.

Then, in the summer of 1678, occurred what was
known as the Popish Plot. This plot was probably
largely invented by a man named Titus Oates, who
claimed that he had discovered evidence that the
Catholics intended to seize the government of
England, kill the king and the leading statesmen,
set fire to the shipping on the Thames, at a given
signal murder all the Protestants, and seize Ireland
with a French army. The people were so excited
that they were willing to believe even such a wild
story as Titus Oates told them, and immediately
the authorities began to arrest and imprison Catholics as zealously as they had been imprisoning

Quakers. The Quakers kept out of the dispute between the Church of England and the Catholics as well as they could, following the advice of Penn, who told his people to keep away from all worldly controversies. "Fly as for your lives," he wrote them in a letter, "from the snares therein, and get you into your watch-tower, the name of the Lord." He urged the Protestants to treat the followers of other creeds more fairly, trying to show them that in their persecution of others the Protestants were themselves guilty of doing the very things which they had most feared from others.

Penn could advise others to keep out of worldly discussions, but he found it hard to do so himself. His nature was too bold and energetic, and he was above all things else a public man. So he tried to help his friend Algernon Sydney win a seat in the House of Commons, and, as a Whig, used all his influence to win success for that party in the elections. Sydney was defeated, but William Penn now became known as something of a politician as well as a religious leader.

In 1680 Penn began to work out a plan that had been in the minds of George Fox and other Quakers for some time, namely, to obtain from the king a grant of land in America where the Quakers might establish a settlement for themselves. They had

already seen the Puritans cross the Atlantic and
found the colony of Massachusetts Bay, where they
were free to establish their own religion, and they
had seen the Catholics go to Maryland under the
guidance of Lord Baltimore. The Quakers were
having a hard time of it at home; why should they
not choose a new land where they could do as they
pleased? They were not welcome in Massachusetts, where some of them had been hung and some
whipped at the tail of a cart. Virginia was being
settled by members of the Church of England,
Maryland by the Catholics, and the Dutch were in
possession of New York. They looked about to
find some territory not yet well occupied.

Some time earlier George Fox had considered
founding a Quaker colony in the country lying
north of Maryland and west of New York and the
Jerseys. Travelers reported that this was easy
to reach by a broad river called the Delaware.
Penn already knew a good deal about this and the
neighboring country, partly from George Fox,
and partly because he had already acted as arbi-
trator in a dispute as to the boundary line between
East Jersey and West Jersey. He had also helped
to draw up the constitution for West Jersey, and,
as that constitution established religious liberty in
that territory, many Quakers had gone there to

live. Indeed, West Jersey might have become a great Quaker colony had it not been that men who went out there reported that its soil was not so fertile nor its general character so attractive as the land that lay farther to the west.

In spite of the difficulties he had so often experienced with the law courts, Penn was now looked upon with favor by both King Charles and his brother the Duke of York. His father, Sir William, had never been paid all the money that was due him as a naval officer; the government was therefore in debt to Penn to the amount of £16,000, and Penn knew that the king was always hard pressed for money to keep up his very expensive court. Penn knew also that the king would make difficulties about paying him the money that was owed, but he thought that Charles might be glad to give him some of the unoccupied land in North America in place of payment in money. Therefore he now, in 1680, sent a petition to King Charles asking that in payment of the money owed to his father he be granted a tract of land "bounded on the east by the Delaware River, on the west limited as Maryland, and northward to extend as far as plantable."

The petition was referred to a committee of the Privy Council, where much discussion followed as to whether such a grant would not conflict with other grants to some of the New England colonies. There was much confusion in the plans, and great doubt as to the boundaries of Maryland. But when the grant was finally made to Penn, it covered a vast stretch of territory, including more than forty thousand square miles of land, the largest grant that had ever been made to one person in America. The tract was larger than Ireland, and not very much smaller than all of England. One reason for such liberality on the part of the king may have been that it canceled a debt of considerable money; another reason was that Charles was particularly well disposed toward the son of his friend Admiral Penn.

Now let us learn how our great State of Pennsylvania was named. On March 4, 1681, the king signed the charter. Penn wrote, "This day my country was confirmed to me under the great seal of England, with large powers and privileges, by the name of Pennsylvania; a name the King would give it in honor of my father. I chose New Wales, being as this is a pretty hilly country, but Penn being Welsh for a head, as Pennanmoire in Wales, and Penrith in Cumberland, and Penn in Buckinghamshire, the highest land in England, called this Pennsylvania, which is the high or head woodlands;

for I proposed when the secretary, a Welshman, refused to have it called New Wales, Sylvania, and they added Penn to it; and though I much opposed it, and went to the King to have it struck out and altered, he said it was past and would take it upon him; nor could twenty guineas move the under secretary to vary the name; for I feared lest it should be looked on as a vanity in me, and not as a respect in the King, as it truly was, to my father, whom he often mentions with praise."

So, in spite of William Penn's modesty, the new colony was christened, as it were by chance, one of the most beautiful names in all the new continent.

Penn owned the new colony much as the lord of an English manor owns his estate. The land belonged to him, and the colonists were in reality to be his tenants, paying him rent for their right to use the land. Penn, on his part, was to pay two beaver skins to the king each year at his castle of Windsor, and the king was also to have one fifth of all the gold and silver that might be found in Pennsylvania.

The charter set forth the form of government for the province. The people were to elect delegates who should pass laws, and Penn was to have the right to veto such laws as he did not approve. He had the right to appoint judges and other officers and to grant pardons for crimes. He was to be the perpetual governor of the province, but if he chose to remain in England, he might govern the colony by a deputy whom he should send out in his place.

A month after the charter was granted to him Penn sent his cousin, William Markham, who was a son of Admiral Penn's sister, to Pennsylvania, to take temporary charge of the few scattered families of Swedes, English, and Dutch, who were living along the shores of the Delaware. Markham arrived at the colony in July, 1681, and established his home at Upland, a settlement some fifteen miles below the site of the present city of Philadelphia. Markham examined the province, and sent word to Penn that Lord Baltimore disputed the boundary lines between Maryland and Pennsylvania, and that, if his claim was correct, Maryland would cut into a large section of southern Pennsylvania. Penn then went to the Duke of York and secured from him an additional grant that gave him land now forming part of the state of Delaware. What he wanted was to obtain control of the entire western shore of the Delaware River from his province down to the Atlantic Ocean.

Then he advertised for settlers for his new domain, warning them that, for a few years at least,

they would have to do without some of the com-
forts of England, but explaining that it was a
glorious opportunity to spread English influence in
a new world. He offered them very easy terms of
rent; they could have five thousand acres by paying £100, and a shilling rent for every hundred
acres annually afterward. If they did not have
the money to take up so large a tract of land, they
could have two hundred acres or less for the rent
of one shilling an acre. These terms were very
attractive, and many persons who were eager to
take a share in what Penn was pleased to call "his
holy experiment of Pennsylvania," applied for
tracts of land in the new colony.

Penn was now a very practical, businesslike man,
and he meant to add to his fortune by means of
his new province, and also to become a man of
great influence. He intended to show that a people like the Quakers could build up a community
where liberty should be the watchword, where war
should be frowned upon, and where every man
should have a chance to own land and cultivate it.
He was not a dreamer only, but a great planner
and organizer as well, one of those men who seized
the opportunity that the new world of America
presented, and hoped that he might there set
right the wrongs that had brought so much trouble

to the poorer classes in Europe. There was probably no finer type of man among those who settled
the colonies of North America than this broad-
minded, well-balanced, shrewd, and yet ideal-
loving Quaker courtier, with his profound sense of
justice, and his determination to deal fairly by all,
— both settlers and Indians.

Some men came to him offering to form a company and pay him £6000 in return for a monopoly
of the trade with the Indians in his province, but
this he refused. He had his own ideas as to how
he and his settlers must deal with the Indians;
they must deal with them fairly; and since they
were to take land that belonged to the Indians,
they must pay for every acre they occupied in their
settlements and farms. This was a new idea, and
not the usual custom, since most colonists paid no
regard whatever to any right the Indians might
have to their lands. He wrote out a set of rules
for dealing with the Indians, and among them it
was stated that a white man who injured an
Indian was to be dealt with exactly as if he had
injured another white man; and that all disputes
between the two races were to be adjusted by a
jury of twelve men, six settlers and six Indians.
A man who tried to obtain some special privileges
from him paid him the following noble tribute: "I

believe he truly does aim more at justice and righteousness, and spreading of truth, than at his own particular gain."

Meantime, several ships carrying settlers started for America, and Penn sent out three agents to choose a site for a town and deal with the Indians of the neighborhood. He told these agents to examine the different creeks on the Pennsylvania side of the Delaware River in order to choose one that should allow boats to go up into the country. To use his own words, he ordered them, "to settle a great town, and be sure to make your choice where it is most navigable, high, dry, and healthy; that is, where most ships may best ride, of deepest draught of water, if possible to load or unload at the bank or quay side, without boating or lighterage."

When the agents arrived, they found that the settlers already there knew the best situation for a great settlement, — at a place a few miles north of where the Schuylkill River flowed into the Delaware. This place they named Philadelphia, a word that means "Brotherly love."

What pleasure and satisfaction Penn must have taken in planning how this new town should be built! He outlined it very carefully, directing where the markets and storehouses should be placed, and telling his agents to choose a site in the center of the line of houses facing the river for his own residence. "Let every house be placed," he suggested, "if the person pleases, in the middle of its plat, as to the breadth of it, that so there may be ground on each side for gardens, or orchards, or fields, that it may be a green country town, which will never be burnt and always wholesome." From that comes the name of "Penn's green country town" that was so often applied to Philadelphia in the early years of its existence.

Penn sent a special letter to the Indians. "Now the great God hath been pleased to make me concerned in your part of the world, " he wrote them, "and the King of the country where I live hath given me a great province therein; but I desire to enjoy it with your love and consent, that we may always live together as neighbors and friends; else what would the great God do to us who hath made us (not to devour and destroy one another, but) to live soberly and kindly together in the world?"

Penn was now such a prominent figure in England, the owner of a great tract of land given him by the king, that he was able to help those Quakers who got into trouble with the government; and when he was not busy planning his colony, he was usually helping some persecuted members of his faith, and urging them to join him in his new province where liberty in religion was to be the keynote. He also drew up a constitution for Pennsylvania, and then, in the summer of 1682, he was ready to set sail for his new domain.

PENN'S SEAL.

CHAPTER VIII

THE proprietor of the new province sailed from Deal, in England, on August 30, 1682, leaving his wife and children at their home in the country. His ship was the *Welcome* and carried about one hundred passengers. The voyage across the Atlantic took nearly two months, for it was the 24th day of October when the *Welcome* sighted the capes of the Delaware. During the voyage thirty of the passengers died of smallpox, a common sickness for a ship to carry in those days.

The *Welcome* took three days to sail up the Delaware to New Castle, which was the chief settlement thereabouts. This place was in the territory that had been granted to Penn by the Duke of York, and here the agents of the duke gave the title to the land to its new owner in their master's name by the old ceremony of "turf and twig and water," a custom long continued in Pennsylvania, and which meant that the former owner, by giving the new owner a piece of turf, a bit of twig, and a

68

cup of water, transferred to him full possession of whatever was to be found on the land in question.

After this ceremony Penn sailed on up the river to the small village of Upland, where his agent, William Markham, was waiting for him. When he had landed at Upland, he asked his friend Pearson to choose a name for the town there, and Pearson, who hailed from the town of Chester in England, gave the settlement the name of that English place.

From Chester William Penn began to explore his new possessions. He found a soil that was rich, woods and fields filled with animals and birds of many kinds, and a wide river with many tributary streams that led far into the interior of his province. Along the Delaware wild birds were plentiful, and every day Indians brought deer from the forests and sold them to the settlers for small amounts of tobacco. The settlers who were already living in the clearings along the Delaware were chiefly Swedes and Dutch, with a few English, who fished in the river, hunted in the bays, and pastured their cattle in the open meadows along the river banks.

Penn was rowed in a barge up the Delaware past a place called Old Tinicum, which had been the residence of the Swedish governor, past that point where the Schuylkill joins the Delaware at what

is now League Island, and on to a stretch where
the Delaware grew narrower and deeper and where
there was high land with a good frontage for deep-
draft boats. Here the shore was covered with
pines, chestnuts, walnuts, oaks, and laurel, and a
small stream flowed into the river. This was the
place that Penn's commissioners had chosen for the
site of his city. He landed at the mouth of the
small stream called Dock Creek, which to-day flows
into the sewer under Dock Street, on the water
front of Philadelphia, and where then stood a log
tavern known as " The Sign of the Blue Anchor."
Tradition says that some English settlers and Indians were on the shore to greet the new owner, and
that he sat down with the Indians and ate the
hominy and roasted acorns that they offered him.
Then they indulged in some athletic sports for
his entertainment, and Penn himself took part in a
jumping match. Tradition has it that he out-
jumped the best of the natives !

He liked the site of his "green country town"
very much, and also the plans that had been made
by his agents. Some of the names they had given
to streets he changed. He altered Pool to Walnut
and Winn to Chestnut Street, because of the trees
that grew near those thoroughfares. One of the
main roads he named High Street, which was later

changed to Market Street. He planned the open
square at Broad and Market streets where the
City Hall now stands, but he intended to have it
include ten acres of ground. He left a wide
boulevard along the Delaware River, and staked
out the city on the plan of a checkerboard, leaving
four open spaces, which were later given the names
of Washington, Franklin, Rittenhouse, and Logan
squares.

Hardly had Penn outlined the map of what he
hoped his little village of Philadelphia would grow
to be, than he set about planning for the education
of the people he was urging to follow him from
Europe. He had induced William Bradford, a
printer of Leicester, England, to make the sea
voyage with him, and set up a printing-press in
the province. In December, 1683, Enoch Flower
opened a school in a two-room shack built of pine
and cedar planks, and six years later a public
school was founded, to be known in time as the
William Penn Charter School, destined to continue
to the present day. Although the post office had
existed in England for only a few years, Penn
thought it so valuable that he issued orders to
have a post office installed in his province with
deliveries once a week, and letters were sent at
the very reasonable cost of twopence from Philadel-

phia to Chester and sixpence from Philadelphia to Maryland.

The first frame building that had been completed in Philadelphia was the "Blue Anchor," which was at one and the same time an inn, an exchange, a corn market, a post office, and a landing-place. It stood fronting the river, and was built of heavy rafters of wood and bricks that were brought from England. The colonists were men of energy and resource; they built substantial houses rapidly, and before long residences with pointed roofs, balconies, and porches were common sights, while an enterprising man named Carpenter built a quay three hundred feet long, where a ship of five hundred tons could be moored. Penn was justly proud of the achievements of his colonists. To Lord Halifax he wrote, "I must without vanity say, I have led the greatest colony into America that ever any man did on private credit; " while to Lord Sunderland he said, "With the help of God and such noble friends, I will show a province in seven years equal to her neighbor's of forty years' planting."

When he had started men to work on his new city, Penn traveled through West and East Jersey, saw Long Island, and incidentally stopped and preached to any Quakers he found in that part of North America. It used to be supposed that he made his famous treaty with the Indians at Kensington at about that time, but historians now believe that it was not made until the following year.

As soon as his new government was in order, the owner of the province of Pennsylvania, accompanied by his council, went to Maryland to discuss the boundary line with Lord Baltimore. The two proprietors met at West River, but could reach no satisfactory adjustments. Then Penn returned to his own colony and spent the winter in the little settlement of Chester. By this time other ships were bringing Quakers to Pennsylvania; twenty-three vessels had arrived within a short time, and their passengers were made very welcome by the settlers who were already established. The young proprietor — he was only thirty-eight years old — must have enjoyed his experience in his new country, if we may judge from his letters. He wrote to his wife, "O how sweet is the quiet of these parts, freed from the anxious and troublesome solicitations, hurries, and perplexities of woeful Europe!" And again he wrote, "I like it so well that a plentiful estate, and a great acquaintance on the other side, have no charms to remove; my family being once fixed with me, and if no other thing occur, I am like to be an adopted American."

In the spring he was very busy overseeing the building of the houses of Philadelphia, and moved from Chester to what was known as the Letitia House in Philadelphia. This house had been built for him facing the river south of what is now Market Street, in a lot that contained about half a city block. The house was built of brick and was later given by Penn to his daughter Letitia.

THE LETITIA HOUSE.

While the newly arrived settlers were building their frame houses, they lived in huts of bark and turf, and some even in caves excavated in the steeper parts of the river bank. There was none of the famine and illness, and few of the hardships, that attended the early settlements in Massachusetts and Virginia. There was plenty of game to be had in the woods and along the river, stone for buildings was plentiful, and the clay beds under the soil provided material for bricks. The colony was comfortable and prosperous, and Penn's system of government had been so well planned that laws were made and enforced with very little friction.

Sometimes Penn himself presided over the meetings of the Provincial Council, which frequently sat as a court of law. One of the early trials was for witchcraft among the Swedes, and was handled so quickly and decisively that the old superstition was prevented from spreading among the people, as it did in Massachusetts a little later. Penn charged the jury, which brought in a verdict that the prisoner was "guilty of the common fame of being a witch; but not guilty in manner and form as she stands indicted." As this amounted to deciding that the prisoner was not guilty of having done any wrong, in spite of her reputation for dealing in witchcraft, a precedent was set which showed that Pennsylvania was to be fair in dealing with all kinds of men and women.

Every one is familiar with Benjamin West's famous picture of Penn making a treaty with the

Indians under the great elm at Kensington. That
scene, however, like many other striking scenes
in history, seems to rest on vague tradition rather
than on facts. There is no exact record of his
first treaty with the Indians, but the place where it
was made is generally supposed to have been on the
bank of the Delaware River near the foot of what
is now called Shackamaxon Street in Philadelphia.
This treaty was simply an agreement as to the
method of buying the land and how it should be
surveyed. Later, deeds were drawn up for the
actual transfer of the lands, and the tracts to be
transferred were surveyed by the old method of
walking against time. Thus it was agreed that
what was known as the Neshaminy tract should
reach beyond the mouth of the Neshaminy Creek
"as far as a man could walk and back in three
days."

How this was done was described by John Wat-
son. "Governor Penn," said he, "with several
Friends and a party of Indians, began in the month
of November at the mouth of the Neshaminy and
walked up the Delaware. In a day and a half
they arrived at a point about thirty miles distant
at the mouth of a creek which they called 'Baker's'
(from the name of the man who first reached it).
Here they marked a spruce tree; and Governor

Penn decided that this was as much land as would be immediately wanted for settlement, and walked no farther. They walked at leisure, the Indians sitting down sometimes to smoke their pipes and the white men to eat biscuit and cheese. . . . A line was afterward run from the spruce tree to Neshaminy and marked, the remainder was left to be walked out when wanted for settlement."

This unusual method of measuring land appears to have been fair enough, at least as long as William Penn was in authority over the white settlers. The Indians had already learned that they could trust him, and found no cause for raising the war-cry against the "Children of Mignon" (Elder Brother), as the followers of William Penn were called. Half a century later, however, when William Penn's son Thomas was the governor, the Lenni-Lenape, or Delaware Indians, from whom Penn had bought much land, became uneasy at the encroachments of some of the settlers, and asked to have a distance, stated in the old agreement to be "as far as a man can go in a day and a half," definitely determined. Thomas Penn, the governor of Pennsylvania, and the chiefs of the Delawares agreed that the distance should be determined by a walk to take place on September 19, 1737. Very early on that morning a large number of colonists gathered at the crossroads near the Friends' meetinghouse at Wrightstown in Pennsylvania.

A large chestnut tree stood at the crossroads, and this was the center of interest for the white men and for the Indians who joined them there. "Ready!" commanded Sheriff Smith, and at the word three white men stepped out from the crowd and put their right hands on the chestnut tree. The three were James Yeates, a New Englander, described as "tall, slim, of much ability and speed of foot"; Solomon Jennings, "a remarkably stout and strong man," and Edward Marshall, a well-known hunter, who was over six feet tall, and noted as a great walker.

Governor Thomas Penn had promised to give five pounds in money and five hundred acres of land to the walker who should cover the greatest distance, and these three had entered the contest for the prize. As the sheriff gave the word to start the three men were off. Yeates took the lead, followed by Jennings, beside whom walked two Indians to see that the walking was fair. After them came men on horseback, among whom were the sheriff and the surveyor general, and at a little distance Governor Thomas Penn himself. At the back of the procession came Edward Marshall,

walking easily, swinging a hatchet in his hand,
"to balance himself," as he said, and munching
dry biscuits that he took from his pocket. He
had said in advance that he would "win the
prize of five hundred acres of land, or lose his life
in the attempt," but he walked as if he had for-
gotten that determination.

The walkers pushed steadily on, never at a loss
for direction, for Thomas Penn had secretly sent
out a surveying party in advance to blaze the trees
along a straight line for as great a distance as it
was thought possible for a man to walk in eighteen
hours. Therefore even when they reached the
wilderness the walkers had the straightest course
marked out for them. Then the Indians began to
protest against the increasing speed of the white
men, saying again and again, "That's not fair.
You are running! You were to *walk.*" In answer
the white men only said that the treaty had used
the words, "As far as a man can *go,*" and therefore they had a right to run if they wished. Presently the Indians tried to delay the march by
stopping to rest, but the horsemen who were with
the party dismounted and insisted on the Indians
riding their horses, and so the "march" continued
as rapidly as ever. At last the Indians refused to
go any farther, and left the white men.

Solomon Jennings was tired out before the
Lehigh River was reached, and left the race to the
other two, following for a time with some of the
spectators.

That night the walking party slept on the north
side of the Lehigh Mountains. In the morning
some of the white men hunted for the horses that
had strayed from camp during the night, while
others went to the village to ask the chief to send
other Indians to accompany the white walkers.
The chief answered angrily, "You have all the
good land now, and you may as well take the bad,
too." Another Indian, who had heard how the
white men had raced along, trying to get as much
land as possible, said disgustedly, "No sit down to
smoke; no shoot squirrel; but lun, lun, lun, all
day long!"

The last half-day's walk had hardly begun when
James Yeates dropped out, finding the exertion of
such a rapid pace too much for him. Marshall,
however, still pressed on, traveling very fast.
When he passed the last of the trees that had been
blazed to guide them, he took a compass held out to
him by the surveyor general, who was riding, and
kept his direction by its aid. At last the sheriff,
looking at his watch, called out, "Halt!" Marshall threw himself forward, and grasped a sapling.

That point then became the mark for the northern
boundary of the purchase made many years before,
a mark that was sixty-eight miles from the chestnut tree at the crossroads at Wrightstown, and
close to the site of the present town of Mauch
Chunk. The distance covered had been twice
as great as the Indians had supposed it would
be.

In another way also the Delawares, who knew
little of legal matters, were tricked by Thomas
Penn's officers. The deed that set forth the
purchase did not state in what direction the
northern boundary was to be drawn, but the
Indians had naturally expected that it would be
run to the nearest point on the Delaware River.
The surveyor general, however, decided that the
line should be drawn at right angles to the direction of the walk, which was almost straight north-
west. If a line were drawn from the town of
Mauch Chunk to the Delaware so that if it were
extended it would reach New York City, that line
would represent what the Indians thought the
northern boundary should be. But if a line be
drawn from Mauch Chunk to the point where New
York, New Jersey, and Pennsylvania meet, the
result will be the boundary that Thomas Penn's
surveyor general actually marked out four days

after Edward Marshall finished his remarkable walk. As a result the amount of land that was taken from the Indians under this purchase was increased from the three hundred thousand acres they thought they should give to half a million acres, and all because white men took a selfish advantage of a loosely worded deed!

The Delawares, or Lenni-Lenape, had always trusted William Penn, because he had been scrupulously fair with them. They had said, "We will live in love with William Penn and his children as long as the sun and moon shall shine." The result of this "Walking Purchase" in 1737, however, which took away from the tribe all the land along the river from which they took their name, was to embitter them against the white men, and destroy the friendship that William Penn had been so careful to create between the two races.

It is pleasant to remember that the settlers of William Penn's time paid the Indians when they made purchases of land. There is a record of the sale of what was called the "Salem tract," a piece of land with a frontage of twenty-four miles on the Delaware and extending back far enough to include over eight hundred square miles. For this, it is related, the Indians received the following curious assortment of articles in payment:

"30 match-coats, 20 guns, 30 kettles, 1 great kettle, 30 pair of hose, 20 fathoms of duffels, 30 petticoats, 30 narrow hoes, 30 bars of lead, 15 small barrels of powder, 70 knives, 30 Indian axes, 70 combs, 60 pair of tobacco tongs, 60 pair of scissors, 60 tinshaw looking-glasses, 120 awl-blades, 120 fish-hooks, 2 grasps of red paint, 120 needles, 60 tobacco boxes, 120 pipes, 200 bells, 100 Jew's-harps, and 6 ankers of rum."

A great deal of oratory was expended on the making of these treaties. Penn wrote of one of them, "When the purchase was agreed, great promises passed between us, of kindness and good neighbourhood, and that the Indians and English must live in love as long as the sun gave light: which done, another made a speech to the Indians, in the name of all the Sachamakan, or kings, first to tell them what was done; next, to charge and command them to love the Christians, and particularly live in peace with me and the people under my government; that many governors had been in the river, but that no governor had come himself to live and stay here before; and having now such an one that had treated them well, they should never do him or his any wrong. At every sentence of which they shouted, and said, Amen, in their way."

Usually in making these treaties a belt of wampum was given to an Indian with an injunction to

remember a certain clause of the agreement, so
that when the Indians wished to refresh their
minds in regard to any of the treaties, they would
gather together, and as each displayed his belt of
wampum he would recite the agreement that the
white men had made when they gave the belt to the
native.

PENN'S WAMPUM BELT.

In general, William Penn's treaties simply promised that the Indians should be fairly treated, and
that they should have redress from the colony's
government in case any settler cheated them.
Similar treaties had been made between the settlers
and the natives for years in that neighborhood and
in other parts of North America. The only thing
that made Penn's treaties really remarkable was
that the Quaker proprietor actually kept his promises. The Indians came to regard this as remarkable, after they had dealt with other white men,
and spread the word that Penn, or Onas, as the
Iroquois called him, or Mignon, as the Delawares
called him, was really a man of his word. In
time this unusual reputation of William Penn

spread across the sea to England and to France. In both countries the reputation for dealing honestly with the Indians caused great surprise, mixed, fortunately, with great admiration for the white governor. Voltaire, the famous French writer, said of Penn's agreement, "This was the only treaty between these people and the Christians that was not ratified by an oath and that was never broken."

CHAPTER IX

WHAT PENN FOUND IN AMERICA

DURING his stay in Pennsylvania William Penn wrote often to his family and friends in England. These letters give us a vivid picture of the new world of America, for they were written by a very keen observer and an unusually well-educated man. They show us the virgin country from which were to grow the homes of a new nation.

"I find the country wholesome," he wrote, "land, air, and water good, divers good sorts of wood and fruits that grow wild, of which plums, peaches and grapes are three; also cedar, chestnut and black walnut and poplar, with five sorts of oak, black and white, Spanish, red and swamp oak the most durable of all, the leaf like the English willow.

"We have laid out a town a mile long, and two miles deep. On each side of the town runs a navigable river, the least as broad as the Thames at Woolwich, the other about a mile over. I think we have near about eighty houses built, and about three hundred farmers settled around the town. I fancy it already pleasanter than the Weald of Kent, our being clearer, and the country not much closer; a coach might be driven twenty miles end-ways. We have had fifty

86

sail of ships and small vessels, since the last summer in our river, which shows a good beginning."

Penn was very proud of the natural riches of his new country.

"Here is a hickory-nut tree," he wrote, "mighty large, and more tough than our ash, the finest white and flaming fire I have ever seen. I have had better venison, bigger, more tender, and as fat as in England. Turkeys of the wood, 8 had of forty and fifty pounds weight. Fish in abundance hereaways yet as I hear of, but oysters, that are monstrous for bigness, though there be a lesser sort."

The climate was a matter of the greatest interest to him.

"For the seasons of the year," he said, "having by God's goodness now lived over the coldest and hottest that the oldest liver in the province can remember, I can say something to an English understanding.

"First of the fall, for then I came in. I found it from the 24th of October to the beginning of December, as we have it usually in England in September, or rather like an English mild spring. From December to the beginning of the month called March, we had sharp frosty weather; not foul, thick, black weather, as our northeast winds bring with them in England, but a sky as clear as in the summer, and the air dry, cold, piercing, and hungry; yet I remember not that I wore more clothes than in England. The reason of this cold is given from the great lakes, which are fed by the fountains of Canada. The winter before was as mild, scarce any ice at all, while this for a few days froze up our great

river Delaware. From that month to the month called
June we enjoyed a sweet spring; no gusts, but gentle showers
and a fine sky. Yet this I observe, that the winds here, as
there, are more inconstant, spring and fall, upon that turn
of nature, than in summer or winter. From thence to this
present month, August, which endeth the summer, commonly speaking, we have had extraordinary heats, yet miti-
gated sometimes by cool breezes."

Penn found the Indians as yet unspoiled by
traffic with the settlers, and his opinion of them
must stand as one of the very best ever given. He
wrote:

"They are generally tall, straight, well built, and of
singular proportion; they tread strong and clever, and
mostly walk with a lofty chin. Of complexion black, but
by design, as the gypsies in England. They grease themselves with bear's fat clarified; and using no defense against
sun and weather, their skins must needs be swarthy. Their
eye is little and black, not unlike a straight-looked Jew.
The thick lip and flat nose, so frequent with the East
Indians and blacks, are not common to them; for I have
seen as comely European-like faces among them, of both
sexes, as on your side the sea; and truly an Italian complexion hath not much more of the white; and the noses
of several of them have as much of the Roman.

"Their language is lofty, yet narrow; but, like the
Hebrew in signification, full. Like short-hand in writing,
one word serveth in the place of three, and the rest are
supplied by the understanding of the hearer; imperfect in
their tenses, wanting in their moods, participles, adverbs,

conjunctions, interjections. I have made it my business to understand it, that I might not want an interpreter on any occasion; and I must say that I know not a language spoken in Europe, that hath words of more sweetness or greatness, in accent and emphasis, than theirs; for instance, Octocockon, Rancocas, Oricton, Shak, Marian, Poquesian, all which are names of places, and have grandeur in them. . . .

"Of their customs and manners there is much to be said. I will begin with children. So soon as they are born they wash them in water, and while very young, and in cold weather to choose, they plunge them in the rivers to harden and embolden them. Having wrapt them in a clout, they lay them on a straight thin board a little more than the length and breadth of the child, and swaddle it fast upon the board to make it straight; wherefore all Indians have flat heads; and thus they carry them at their backs. The children will go very young, at nine months commonly. They wear only a small clout round their waist till they are big. If boys, they go a-fishing till ripe for the woods, which is about fifteen. Then they hunt; and, having given some proofs of their manhood by a good return of skins, they may marry: else it is a shame to think of a wife. The girls stay with their mothers, and help to hoe the ground, plant corn, and carry burthens; and they do well to use them to that, while young, which they must do when they are old; for the wives are the true servants of the husbands: otherwise the men are very affectionate to them. . . .

"Their houses are mats or barks of trees, set on poles in the fashion of an English barn, but out of the power of the winds, for they are hardly higher than a man. They lie on reeds or grass. In travel they lodge in the woods about a great fire, with the mantle of duffils " [a coarse woolen cloth] "they wear by day wrapt about them, and a few boughs stuck round them.

"Their diet is maize or Indian corn divers ways prepared, sometimes roasted in the ashes, sometimes beaten and boiled with water, which they call homine. They also make cakes not unpleasant to eat. They have likewise several sorts of beans and peas that are good nourishment : and the woods and rivers are their larder. . . .

"But in liberality they excel. Nothing is too good for their friend. Give them a fine gun, coat, or other thing, it may pass twenty hands before it sticks : light of heart, strong affections, but soon spent : the most merry creatures that live : they feast and dance perpetually; they never have much, nor want much. Wealth circulateth like the blood. All parts partake; and though none shall want what another hath, yet exact observers of property. Some kings have sold, others presented, me with several parcels of land. The pay or presents I made them were not hoarded by the particular owners; but the neighboring kings and their clans being present when the goods were brought out, the parties chiefly concerned consulted what, and to whom, they should give them. To every king, then, by the hands of a person for that work appointed, is a proportion sent, so sorted and folded, and with that gravity which is admirable. Then that king subdivided it in like manner among his dependents, they hardly leaving themselves an equal share with one of their subjects : and be it on such occasions as festivals, or at their common meals, the kings distribute, and to themselves last. They care for little, because they want but little : and the reason is, a little contents them. In this they are sufficiently revenged on us. If they are ignorant of our pleasures, they are also free from our pains.

They are not disquieted with bills of lading and exchange, nor perplexed with Chancery suits and Exchequer reckonings. We sweat and toil to live. Their pleasure feeds them; I mean their hunting, fishing, and fowling, and this table is spread everywhere."

It would have been fortunate for settlers in other colonies if they had taken the same friendly view of the Indians that Penn did, and, finding the natives a different race from themselves, had made allowances for those differences.

As Penn was on good terms with the Indians so he was with the men of other races who had settled near his province. He liked the Dutch and the Swedes as well as the English. He wrote of those who had located in his territory:

"The first planters in these parts were the Dutch, and soon after them the Swedes and Finns. The Dutch applied themselves to traffic, the Swedes and Finns to husbandry. There were some disputes between them for some years; the Dutch looking upon them as intruders upon their purchase and possession, which was finally ended in the surrender made by John Rizeing, the Swedish Governor, to Peter Stuyvesant, Governor for the States of Holland, anno 1655.

"The Dutch inhabit mostly those parts of the province that lie upon or near the Bay, the Swedes the Freshes [1] of the River Delaware.

[1] The "Freshes" of the Delaware were the low-lying meadows along the river. The Swedes built their homes on the upland

"There is no need of giving any description of them, who are better known there than here; but they are a plain, strong, industrious people, yet have made no great progress in culture, or propagation of fruit-trees; as if they desired rather to have enough than plenty or traffic. . . . They kindly received me as well as the English, who were few before the people connected with me came among them. I must needs commend their respect to authority, and kind behavior to the English. They do not degenerate from the old friendship between both kingdoms. As they are people proper and strong of body, so they have fine children, and almost every house full: rare to find one of them without three or four boys and as many girls; some six, seven, and eight sons. And I must do them that right, I see few young men more sober and laborious."

It was in the summer of 1683 when Penn had written home that fifty vessels had arrived during the past year, that about eighty houses had been built in Philadelphia, and some three hundred farms were under cultivation in the near neighborhood. It is estimated that about three thousand settlers had now arrived. Penn himself made a long horseback trip into the country, meeting many Indians, living in their wigwams, learning

portions and pastured their cattle in the low lands. Their interest centered on the river which provided them with a seemingly inexhaustible supply of fish and game, and on the rich grass of the river meadows where no trees had to be cleared away to provide pasture-land.

something of their language, and continually gain-
ing their good will and friendship. After this
journey he wrote a long letter to the Free Society
of Traders, in which he described the country in
detail, and gave remarkably accurate accounts of
the trees and flowers, the soil and climate, of his
great province.

He loved an outdoor life, and was so delighted
with his new domain that he planned, and later
built, a country home for himself about twenty
miles above Philadelphia, near where Bristol is
now situated. This place he called Pennsbury.
He did not have a chance to do more than plan it
at this time, for the boundary disputes with Lord
Baltimore had now been referred to the Privy
Council in London, and Penn felt that he must go
there himself to represent his claims, and also to
see his family. So he left his colony on August 16,
1684, sailing in a small ship called a ketch, and
reached England after a seven weeks' voyage.

CHAPTER X

TROUBLOUS DAYS IN ENGLAND

PENN found himself in a curious position when he arrived in England. He was a great man, the governor of a large colony which was reputed to be extraordinarily rich, and at the same time he was one of the leaders of a sect which was once more frowned upon and disliked by both the king and the court. As he himself said, "One day I was received well at court as proprietor and governor of a province of the crown, the next taken up at a meeting by Hilton and Collingwood, and the third smoakt" [smoked out or hunted out] "and informed of for meeting with the men of the whig stamp."

He went to see King Charles and the Duke of York, but, though they were glad to see their former friend, they both now felt that the troubles besetting their government were largely due to dissenting religious parties, and that the Quakers were among the chief of these dissenters. Penn saw that he must not lose the good opinion of the

king if he were to have any success in his dispute
with Lord Baltimore, a nobleman who had great
influence at court; at the same time he found that
many Quakers were being ill-treated for their religion and felt called upon to help them. The
case of one man in particular appealed to him,
Richard Vickris, a quiet man who had been sen-
tenced to execution because he refused to take an
oath and who had broken certain statutes for the
suppression of dissenters. This case Penn appealed
to the Duke of York, and the latter finally secured
Vickris's pardon from the king.

In the midst of this confused state of affairs in
England, the easy-going, pleasure-loving Charles
II. died, and his brother, the Duke of York, became
king as James II. The new king could make fair
promises to his friends, and when William Penn
spoke to him about the Quakers, the king promised
to show all sorts of favors to them. He had a
great deal to say about liberty and about religious
toleration.

When the Quakers sent him a petition for clemency, setting forth that there were then thirteen
hundred of their creed in prison in England, and
that hundreds had died of prison hardships in the
past few years, the king was much concerned, and
showed his concern by setting free all dissenters

who were in prison, including both the Quakers
and the Roman Catholics. Probably the king
thought to strengthen himself on the throne by
this act of clemency; certainly it was providential
for the Quakers who had been separated from their
families and friends for years, and undoubtedly. it
made Penn feel very grateful to his sovereign.

Strange as it may seem, there must have been
a real intimacy between the straightforward and
outspoken Penn and the crafty and double-deal-
ing king. Gerard Croese, who wrote the history
of the early Quakers, dwelt upon this strange
friendship. "William Penn," he quaintly says,
"was greatly in favor with the King—the Quaker's
sole patron at court — on whom the hateful eyes
of his enemies were intent. The king loved him as
a singular and entire friend, and imparted to him
many of his secrets and counsels. He often hon-
ored him with his company in private, discoursing
with him of various affairs, and that, not for one,
but many hours together, and delaying to hear the
best of his peers who at the same time were waiting
for an audience. One of these being envious, and
impatient of delay, and taking it as an affront to
see the other more regarded than himself, adven-
tured to take the freedom to tell his majesty, that
when he met with Penn he thought little of his

nobility. The King made no other reply than that Penn always talked ingenuously, and he heard him willingly."

Then the young Duke of Monmouth raised a rebellion and tried to seize the throne. Many Protestants joined his cause, but he was defeated, and there followed the slaughter of all who had sided with Monmouth, or who were even suspected of siding with him. The cruel Judge Jeffreys went through the country leaving a trail of gibbeted heads and ruined homes behind him, thereby bringing the Catholic king and his court in more disfavor than ever with the great Protestant majority of the people. But Penn did not desert the king, although he must have hated the bloodshed that James tolerated in his officers. "The King," said he, "was much to be pitied, for he was hurried into all this effusion of blood by Jeffreys' impetuous and cruel temper." He advised the Quakers to keep quiet and refrain from mixing in public affairs. And meantime he himself used all his influence to protect those who fell under suspicion of disloyalty to the Crown.

The Quakers were glad enough to have a friend at court, and there was no doubt but that Penn was a very influential man. In those days there were many men with some standing at court who

H

were known as "pardon-brokers"; men whose
business it was to obtain pardons for persons
accused of crimes, usually exacting payment of all
the accused person's wealth in return. Penn used
his influence to obtain pardons only because of his
belief in the innocence of the man or woman under
accusation, and this honesty of his, in an age when
treachery and deceit were the usual standards,
made him more than ever a marked and notable
man.

He soon had so many "clients," as those who
sought favors of an influential man were called,
that he felt obliged to rent Holland House, the
London residence of the Earl of Warwick, and he
had his own coach and four horses, as well as other
luxuries that befitted his position as an intimate
friend of the king. These expenses, and the money
he was continually giving to his needy Quaker
friends, soon began to be a heavy drain on his fortune, and again and again he spoke of wishing he
could move his family to the new home in Pennsylvania, taking up there the simple and free life that
he had enjoyed so much on his first visit. But his
dispute with Lord Baltimore was not yet settled,
and he felt too great a responsibility for the Quakers
in England to leave London then; he doubtless
also enjoyed his new prominence as a courtier; for

Penn, in spite of his Quaker simplicity, was in many ways a man who thoroughly appreciated power and influence and the good report of the world.

Matters of state were growing more and more tangled in England. The king was appointing Roman Catholics to office, and was not as well disposed toward the men of the Church of England as the Protestants thought proper. On all sides men and women were plotting for their own advancement, too often changing their religion to suit their ambitions of the moment. Penn, who would preach to a Quaker meeting, and then go to the king's chambers, where he would meet Catholics and priests, seemed to be acting after the general fashion of the time, but nevertheless his intimacy with the king caused gossip and some suspicions of his motives.

He trod a very difficult path in those days, often seeming to be "carrying water on both shoulders." In the summer of 1686 he made another journey to Holland and Germany, and in the former country Penn went to see William, the Prince of Orange, bearing messages, some historians say, from King James to William. This Prince of Orange had married Mary, the daughter of James II. of England, and Mary was next in line of succession to the English throne. Penn's mission seems to have been to persuade William and Mary that there should be religious freedom in England, as King James had proclaimed it, and to this William, who was an ardent Protestant, was only too glad to agree. But when he found that his father-in-law's religious freedom was likely to end in turning England over to the Pope, he was much less enthusiastic, and did not altogether relish the arguments made to him by the Quaker envoy Penn. William himself believed that Penn was an honest man, perhaps hoodwinked by the clever courtiers around King James, but some other people in Holland were not so sure of this, and suspected Penn of being at heart a Catholic, and even spread that report concerning him. Many of the followers of the Prince of Orange — men who were to go with him to England later when he became king of that country — despised and distrusted the Quaker, and Penn seemed unable to set himself right before them. He was getting deeper and deeper into the toils of his peculiar position, for he wished to show himself a sincere Quaker, yet he appeared to be acting in the interest of the Church of Rome.

In Holland he met some Presbyterian refugees from Scotland, among them Sir Robert Stuart, of Coltness. When he returned to England, Penn

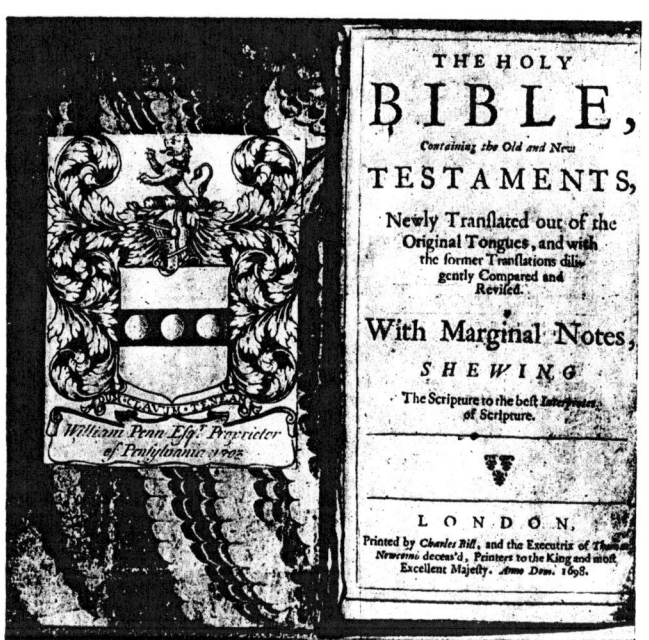

Reproduced from Fisher's "The True William Penn," through the courtesy of the J. B. Lippincott Company.

WILLIAM PENN'S BIBLE AND BOOK-PLATE.

recommended that King James should allow these men to return, since they were in exile solely on account of their religion, and were not guilty of any treason. The king consented, but when Sir Robert Stuart did return, he found that he was penniless, because all his property had been given over to the Earl of Arran. Sir Robert went to Penn and told him the state of affairs. Penn took the matter up at once, and went to the Earl of Arran. The Earl of Buchan has described how Penn managed the matter.

"'Thou hast taken possession of Coltness's estate,' said Penn. 'Thou knowest that it is not thine.'

"'That estate,' said Arran, 'I paid a great price for. I received no other reward for my expensive and troublesome embassy in France.'

"'All very well, friend James, but of this assure thyself, that if thou dost not give me this moment an order on thy chamberlain for two hundred pounds to Coltness to carry him down to his native country, and a hundred a year to subsist on till matters are adjusted, I will make it as many thousands out of thy way with the King.'"

So spoke Penn, and as a result the Earl of Arran complied with Penn's request, and a little later the entire estate was restored to Sir Robert Stuart.

Evidently men understood that William Penn had great influence with the king of England.

When he returned from Holland, Penn found that the Quakers were increasing in numbers, and he often preached to as many as a thousand listeners at a single meeting. At the same time his steward and others in Pennsylvania were writing to him for more money, and he was sending them all he could spare, and more too, although, as he sometimes complained in his letters, he could not see why such a naturally wealthy province should require any help from him. He wrote that he would gladly go out to his province again, if it were not that the boundary dispute with Lord Baltimore kept him in England. But naturally he wanted his people there to make a profit for him out of his great possessions. "If my table, cellar and stable may be provided for," he wrote, "with a barge and yacht or sloop for the service of governor or government, I may try to get hence, for in the sight of God, I can say I am five thousand pounds behind-hand more than I ever received or saw for land in that province, and to be so baffled by the merchants is discouraging and not to be put up."

In 1687, King James issued a Declaration of Indulgence which looked like a wonderful step forward for religious liberty. He abolished the

laws which prevented dissenters and Roman
Catholics from sitting in Parliament or holding
public office. This sounded well, but unfortunately
James, like all the Stuart kings, insisted on acting
of his own accord, without getting either the consent of Parliament or the approval of his people.
Yet, in spite of this defect, the Declaration of Indulgence was gladly accepted by most members
of those sects that had so long been out of favor
with the government, and the Quakers presented
the king with an address, telling him how well his
act was received throughout England. The king
appeared to be pleased with what the Quakers
said, and made them a grateful reply. "Gentle-
men," said he, "I thank you heartily for your
address. Some of you know (I am sure you do,
Mr. Penn,) that it was always my principle, that
consciences ought not to be forced, and that all
men ought to have the liberty of their consciences.
And what I have promised in my declaration I will
continue to perform so long as I live. And I hope
before I die, to settle it, so that after ages shall have
no reason to alter it."

But if the Quakers were pleased at this act of
the king, the Roman Catholics were even more
delighted. Soon it became apparent that the
latter were going to reap the greatest benefit

from this new act of clemency on the part of King James.

As it became evident that the king meant to have his own way, in spite of Parliament or public opinion, and that his way was probably to turn the government over to the followers of the Church of Rome, the dissenters flocked to the aid of the Church of England. Much as Presbyterians, Baptists, Quakers, and other dissenting people disagreed with the English Established Church, they all felt that it was far preferable to the Church of Rome. They knew that King James was hand in glove with the Pope and with the French king, Louis XIV., and they could foresee that if their sovereign should have his way, the country might quickly return to the conditions of the reign of "Bloody Mary." So practically all Protestants now opposed King James's illegal Declaration of Indulgence. But William Penn did not; he said he still trusted the king, and published a pamphlet entitled "Good Advice to Roman Catholic and Protestant Dissenters," in which he supported the king, although he published the pamphlet anonymously. Then he traveled over the country, trying to induce people to agree with his view of James.

The king next tried to seize the universities of Oxford and Cambridge for the Catholics. He

made over to them Christ Church College and
University College at Oxford, and when there was a
vacancy in the office of president of Magdalen
College, he ordered the fellows to elect a Catholic.
The fellows refused, and the king's officers broke
down the college doors, turned out the president
whom the fellows had elected, the fellows themselves, and the students, and turned the place into
a Papal seminary. At first Penn remonstrated
with the king about this, but soon afterward he
changed and advised the college to yield. Here
Penn made a grievous mistake; no wonder people
began to think that the former champion of
religious liberty was no longer a Quaker at heart.

King James went on with his schemes. He was
growing so bold that he tried to run all the counties
and boroughs, and force people to choose his own
favorites for their officers. Wherever he could he
turned out the old officers and put in his Catholic
friends. Then, in April, 1688, he made another
blunder. He issued another Declaration of Indulgence very similar to his first one, and said
that he would appoint no one to public office
except those who would support him in maintain-
ing this indulgence, and then ordered that this new
law should be read on two successive Sundays by
the clergymen in all the churches of England.

He meant in this way to humiliate the Church of England. But James had now gone too far. Only a few clergymen read the new Declaration, and in most cases where they did, the people left the churches as soon as they heard the first words of it. Seven bishops petitioned the king not to enforce his order to have the act read, and King James had these seven tried for libel, and imprisoned them in the Tower of London while they were awaiting trial because they refused to give bail. This was what became famous as the Case of the Seven Bishops, and roused men all over England to the wildest pitch of indignation. Penn opposed this arrest of the seven bishops, but he still acted as a friend of the king and tried to plead his cause.

About the same time a son was born to the king and queen, and the English people thought this meant that the Catholics would secure control of the government for the next reign. They were determined that this should not be, and so they invited William, the Protestant Prince of Orange, and his wife Mary, the daughter of James II., to come and take the throne of England. William landed and took the crown with very little opposition. James, deserted by his court, his army, and his navy, threw the Great Seal of England into the river Thames, and fled to France, where he lived

the remainder of his days in a palace given to him
by Louis XIV.

England was now in a much better way. The
country had an honest king and queen who shortly
proclaimed a religious liberty that was sincere.
But Penn was under a cloud of suspicion. Men
said that King James had sent him to William of
Orange earlier to induce William to side with him
in his Declaration of Indulgence, and men knew now
that he was the author of that pamphlet "Good
Advice to Roman Catholic and Protestant Dissenters" that had attempted to justify King James.
Some of Penn's friends urged him to clear himself
of the charges that were being spread concerning
him. They told him that his own consciousness of
innocence was giving him too great a contempt for
the slanders and gossip that were rife about him.
But in reply Penn only protested his friendship for
James and his belief in the king's fairness, although it had become plain to the rest of the
world that James was an unscrupulous deceiver.

His final reason for his unwavering support of
James lay in these words of his: "To this let me
add the relation my father had to this king's service, his particular favor in getting me released
out of the Tower of London in 1669, my father's
humble request to him upon his death-bed to pro-

tect me from the inconveniences and troubles my
persuasion" [creed] "might expose me to, and his
friendly promise to do it and exact performance
of it from the moment I addressed myself to him;
I say when all this is considered, anybody that has
the least pretence to good nature, gratitude, or
generosity, must needs know how to interpret my
access to the king."

And that was probably the true explanation of
William Penn's devotion to an unjust king, — his
gratitude to a man who had been the friend of
both his father and himself. That same strong
trait of friendship was shown time and again in
Penn's dealings with agents in Pennsylvania who,
relying on his friendship, deceived him. It was,
perhaps, a noble trait; but it placed this Quaker
leader, a man who had fought so long and so
earnestly to secure religious freedom in England, in
the curious position of friend and supporter of a
sovereign who had been doing his best to suppress
liberty of religion. It is small wonder that many
people in England failed to understand Penn's
attitude; and small wonder that, when William and
Mary came to the throne, Penn stood in a dis-
credited and very difficult position.

CHAPTER XI

THE new king of England, William III., was an honest, upright man, and made a fine ruler, in many ways one of the very finest that England has ever had. The government had been very corrupt under the last two Stuart kings; under William and Mary it became respectable. William had already made the small country of the Netherlands a power in the world, and had fought valiantly to defend the Protestant cause. When he became king of the much stronger country of England, he said to a friend, "At last I have a weapon whose blows will hurt!" He meant that he could now do more than ever for religious freedom.

And he did more for religious freedom than any king of England ever had done. He did not make promises only to break them, nor play off one party against another for his own selfish aims. He found the country a very network of intrigue and plotting, and he straightened it out as speedily as he could. He was a colder, more reserved man than

either Charles, the "Merry Monarch," or James
II. had been, and he had of course to make a great
many changes in the government, so that it followed quite naturally that those men who were
used to the two Stuart kings were not altogether
pleased with William. Penn was one of those men;
having been fond of Charles and James, he did not
take kindly to William; and he allowed himself
to appear almost an enemy to the new ruling
house.

Now King William, although he had no particular affection for the Quaker leader, was quite
ready to be perfectly fair with him. He would
probably have been glad to ask Penn's advice in
regard to matters that concerned the Quakers, had
not an unfortunate accident happened which placed
Penn under suspicion. The exiled King James
wrote a letter to Penn from France; and, as King
William's spies were careful to trace all the letters
James sent to England, it soon became known that
Penn had been receiving messages from the exiled
king. The first thing Penn knew he was served
with an order to appear before the Privy Council
and answer to a charge of carrying on a treasonable
correspondence. He was not frightened. He went
at once to the Council, surrendered himself, and
asked that he might be allowed to make his answer

in the presence of the king. This was agreed to, and the meeting was set for the next day.

William was gracious and kindly when the Quaker, hat in hand, appeared before him; and the king alluded to the pleasure he had had in meeting Mr. Penn at the Hague. Then he drew out the letter from King James that his spies had intercepted, and handed it to Penn, saying that the signature was undoubtedly that of James Stuart. He then asked Penn to read the letter aloud. This Penn did, and found that the letter reminded Penn of James's friendship for his father and for himself, and hoped that in its hour of need he would come to the aid of the Stuart cause.

Penn handed the letter back to the king, who asked what King James meant by requesting Penn to come to his aid, and why James had written to him. Penn answered that it was impossible for him to prevent James writing to him, if the late king wished to do so. He then went on to admit that he had loved King James in his prosperity, and could not hate him now in his adversity; that he was willing to repay his kindness in any private way he could; but that he had no thought of disloyalty to the new sovereign, and had never been guilty of any disloyal act. His defense was so manly and frank that William was willing to discharge Penn at once, but, as some of his Council objected, the king ordered William Penn to give bail to appear at the next "Trinity term" of court, which began on May 22 and ended on June 12. When Penn furnished this bail, he was given his liberty.

Soon afterward King William went to Ireland to put down a rebellion that was being led by James and his followers, and in his absence Queen Mary took charge of the affairs of state. She listened to the stories of some men who were doubtless trying to gain her favor by slandering others, and caused the arrest of eighteen prominent men who were charged with conspiring "to restore James Stuart to the throne of England." One of the names on the list was that of William Penn. He was arrested, and again released on bail. The case never came to trial, but these two charges were sufficient to keep him under the eye of the law, and force him to lead a secluded and careful life. Once let a man who had been as prominent and popular as William Penn fall into disfavor and scores of enemies will spring up to steal away his good name. So it was then, and many a time in the years that were to come he must have longed for the free, outdoor life of his colony across the seas where he had been so happy.

After a time he began to plan to return to Pennsylvania, and advertised for more settlers to go out there with him. He was on the point of sailing when he learned by chance that another warrant had been issued for his arrest, and that already the officers were looking for him. Probably he now despaired of clearing his name to the satisfaction of the government; in any event he decided on a new course; he did not give himself up, but instead went into hiding, disappearing as if he were really afraid of trying to prove his innocence.

No one knows exactly what became of Penn during those next three years. Some say that he took private lodgings in London, and explain that the great city was so full of little, hidden courts and narrow, twisting alleys that it was easy for a man to conceal himself there for a long time. Others say that he spent part of that time in France, and it seems likely that much of the time he was on the move, for he himself wrote in a letter, "I have been above these three years hunted up and down, and could never be allowed to live quietly in city or country."

It was a most unfortunate situation for a man who had lived the upright life that William Penn had, and one who had done so much for liberty of conscience. It seems as if Penn must have

I

been afraid of the lying statements of enemies, and feared that their false words would outweigh the truth. There were then a number of men in England who made a good living by being "informers," making up their charges out of whole cloth. Unscrupulous persons sometimes sought the help of such informers to put enemies out of the way. Penn wrote to a meeting of Quakers in London, "My privacy is not because men have sworn truly, but falsely, against me; 'for wicked men have laid in wait for me and false witnesses have laid to my charge things that I knew not.'" He also sent a letter to his friends in Pennsylvania, saying, "By this time thou wilt have heard of the renewal of my troubles, the only hinderance of my return, being in the midst of my preparations with a great company of adventurers when they came upon me. The jealousies of some and unworthy dealings of others have made way for them; but under and over it all the ancient Rock has been my shelter and comfort; and I hope yet to see your faces with our ancient satisfaction."

It hardly seems credible that Penn could have actually conspired against the new king and queen, and yet plots were much in the air in those days, and, as we have already seen, the Quaker leader could be rather easily influenced by people of whom he was fond. In any event, he seems at that time to have been treated as an object of suspicion, and at this distant date it cannot be said positively whether he deserved this suspicion or whether he was the unhappy victim of unscrupulous "informers."

King William left England on a visit to the Hague, and in his absence another plot was discovered, this time to bring James over from France in the king's absence and seize London before the army could be ready to defend it. The plot was discovered before it had made any real headway. Bishop Burnet said, "The men who laid this design were the Earl of Clarendon, the Bishop of Ely, the Lord Preston, and his brother Mr. Graham, and Penn, the famous Quaker."

The first four of these men were really guilty, and one of them, Preston, being actually caught with the papers in his possession, saved his life by turning state's evidence, and in his confession named William Penn as one of the conspirators. So Penn was included in the order for the arrest of all the traitors.

There was nothing to prove Penn guilty, so he simply kept up his policy of hiding. He did, however, send his brother-in-law to Henry Sydney, an old friend of his who was high in favor with King

William. Sydney agreed to meet Penn and hear his side of the matter. The two men met, and afterward Sydney wrote to the king and told him what Penn had said. The sum of this was that Penn was really a loyal subject of William's. He said that he was not plotting and knew of no plot, and only asked that the king would grant him an interview so that he might clear himself.

Being busy in Ireland, the king could not see him at that time, and so Penn kept in concealment. A little later he wrote again to Sydney, urging him to beg the king not to believe all the unjust stories that were being spread concerning him. He said that he only desired to be allowed to live quietly in England or America, and added that the Quakers would vouch for his keeping quiet and doing no harm. He ended by saying that he felt that he had been very much mistreated, and that a less peaceable subject might almost have been driven to conspiracies by such hard usage.

He did not dare, however, to give himself up for trial on any of the charges against him. He felt certain that he could explain away those charges if he might meet the king privately, but he would not stand an open trial in court. He said to Sydney, "Let me be believed and I am ready to appear; but when I remember how they began to use me in Ireland upon corrupt evidence before this business, and what some ill people have threatened here, besides those under temptation, and the providences that have successively appeared for my preservation under this retirement, I can not, without unjustifiable presumption, put myself into the power of my enemies." It is a very strange and mixed-up situation, it being clear that Penn was afraid of what his enemies might show against him, though whether there, was actually any good ground for their charges no one can positively say.

He must have felt uneasy even when hiding in England, for presently he went to France. History does not tell us what he did there, nor how long he remained. In the meantime King William took away from him the government of his province of Pennsylvania, and the rents of his estates in Ireland were declared confiscated.

After some time the fugitive must have thought that the government might have become more friendly to him, for he tried to get Lord Rochester to make his peace with King William. He said that if the king would dismiss the charges against him, he would go back to Pennsylvania, although he would like first to go to Ireland and try to recover some of his ruined estates. There was now

less fear of conspiracies of followers of James II.;
moreover, the government may well have thought
that there was little danger to be feared from Penn;
and that they would be well rid of him if he would
go to Pennsylvania and use his energies in straight-
ening out matters there. Three noblemen, Lords
Rochester, Ranelagh, and Romney, the new title
of his friend Henry Sydney, saw the king on Penn's
behalf. William was willing to be lenient. So
Penn was able to write this interesting letter to his
friends in his American colony:

"This comes by the Pennsylvania Merchant, — Harrison,
commander, and C. Saunders, merchant. By them and
this know, that it hath pleased God to work my enlargement,
by three Lords representing my case as not only hard, but
oppressive; that there was nothing against me but what
impostors, or those that are fled, or that have, since their
pardon refused to verify (and asked me pardon for saying
what they did), alleged against me; that they had long
known me, some of them thirty years, and had never known
me to do an ill thing, but many good offices; and that for
not being thought to go abroad in defiance of the Government, I might and would have done it two years ago; and
that I was, therefore, willing to wait to go about my affairs,
as before, with leave; that I might be the better respected in
the liberty I took to follow it.

"King William answered, 'That I was his old acquaintance, as well as theirs; and that I might follow my business
as freely as ever; and that he had nothing to say to me,' —

upon which they pressed him to command one of them to declare the same to the Secretary of State, Sir John Trench-ard, that if I came to him, or otherwise, he might signify the same to me, which he also did. The Lords were Roches-ter, Ranelagh, and Sydney; and the last, as my greatest acquaintance, was to tell the Secretary; accordingly he did; and the Secretary, after speaking himself, and having it from King William's own mouth, appointed me a time to meet him at home; and did with the Marquis of Winchester, and told me I was as free as ever; and as he doubted not my prudence about my quiet living, for he assured me I should not be molested or injured in any of my affairs, at least while he held that post. The Secretary is my old friend, and one I served after the D. of Monmouth and Lord Russel's busi-ness; I carried him in my coach to Windsor, and presented him to King James; and when the Revolution came, he bought my four horses that carried us. It was about three or four months before the Revolution. The Lords spoke the 25th of November, and he discharged me on the 30th.

"From the Secretary I went to our meeting, at the Bull and Mouth; thence to visit the sanctuary of my solitude; and after that to see my poor wife and children; the eldest being with me all this while. My wife is yet weakly; but I am not without hopes of her recovery, who is of the best of wives and women."

So Penn came out of his hiding and appeared again in the full light of London. We find a man named Narcissus Luttrell writing in his diary for December 5, 1693: "Wm. Penn, the Quaker, having for some time absconded, and having com-

promised the matters against him, appears now in
public, and on Friday last held forth at the Bull
and Mouth in St. Martin's."

As he was always an active, energetic man,
William Penn had been busy writing during the
time of his concealment. He had written a number
of new Quaker pamphlets, and also his famous
collection of maxims called "Fruits of Solitude."
In a wider and more interesting field he had also
written "An Essay towards the Present Peace of
Europe," in which he urged that all disputes
between governments be settled by a court of
arbitration, and that a United States of Europe,
with a general council containing representatives
of each nation, should be formed.

It is said that Penn's devoted wife had gone to
King James and his queen in France every year
since he had lost his throne, and carried them
tokens of devotion from their friends in England.
She was always well received, and even the sup-
porters of William could find little fault in so gracious an act. But Guli Penn said that she did
this from friendship for the exiles, and not through
any opposition to the new rulers of her land.

Soon after Penn was free to live as he pleased
his gentle wife died, leaving three children,
Springett, William, and Letitia. They had been

a devoted couple, and Penn found this loss a very hard one to bear. Difficulties of many sorts beset him. His fortune had been spent in various ways during the troubled days of his fall from favor, and he now looked across the sea, in the hope that he might find in his province of Pennsylvania some of the peace and satisfaction he had known there on his first visit, and had dreamed of from time to time ever since.

CHAPTER XII

KING WILLIAM had taken the government of
Pennsylvania away from William Penn probably
because he thought that a colony governed by a
Quaker friend of James Stuart might easily become
a prey to French greed. But when the king and
Penn became reconciled, the province was given
back to Penn, in August, 1694. Although he was
anxious to see his new city of Philadelphia again,
it was not until five years later that Penn was able
to cross the Atlantic. This was largely due to the
fact that he had very little money left.

His colony of Pennsylvania had cost him a great
deal of money; and, although he had expected
large returns from the land and natural products
there, he found that the colony caused greater and
greater leakage to his purse. The settlers would
not pay even the very small quit-rent of one
shilling a year for each hundred acres, and were
constantly calling on Penn to help them. His
estates in Ireland brought in no profits, and the

property at Worminghurst that had belonged to Mrs. Penn had been left in trust for her oldest son, Springett Penn, who was then about nineteen years old. All that Penn received from that property was enough to support and educate the three children.

While he stayed in England he began preaching again, and found that now, under William and Mary, the Quakers were allowed the fullest liberty to hold their meetings, and that religious persecution was a thing of the past. His preaching was very successful. Wherever he spoke great crowds gathered to hear the words of a man who had had such a remarkable history, who had been a close friend of King James, and who had been in hiding for some years. Penn was unquestionably a very eloquent speaker, and his many experiences must have added very much to the interest of what he had to tell the quiet-living Quakers of the English countryside.

Three years after his first wife died Penn married again, this time Hannah Callowhill, of Bristol. Soon afterward he lost his oldest child, Springett, a boy of great charm and a close companion of his father. Of Guli Penn's two other children, William became dissipated and was a great disappointment to Penn, and Letitia married William

Aubrey, who turned out to be a very disagreeable son-in-law. By his second wife Penn had six children, four of whom, John, Thomas, Margaret, and Richard, ultimately became the joint owners of Pennsylvania.

Penn now moved to the English city of Bristol, where he continued making plans for his province, and preaching and arguing with people who did not approve of his religion. The Quakers were then doing a certain amount of missionary work, and the story goes that Penn sought out a young Russian prince who was studying shipbuilding in England, and gave him Quaker books which he explained to him. In time this prince became the Emperor Peter the Great of Russia, and he is said always to have taken great interest in the Quakers because of what Penn had taught him.

Meantime, much had happened in Pennsylvania. The history of the province had been full of ups and downs, many of its difficulties being due to the fact that for fifteen years Penn had been obliged to stay away from it. There had been many squabbles between the settlers and the men appointed to govern the province, but in spite of disagreements the colony had grown until now there were nearly twenty thousand settlers there.

When Penn left his colony in 1684, he had placed

the power in the charge of a Council of eighteen men, and each of the eighteen had felt that it was his duty to do all the governing. When he learned that this system did not work well, Penn had tried to mend matters by doing away with the Council and appointing five commissioners. But this did not work very well, either, and in less than a year Penn appointed an old soldier of Cromwell's army, Captain John Blackwell, to replace the commissioners, and act as a deputy governor. The Quakers, however, did not like being in charge of a soldier, and made matters so difficult for Captain Blackwell that he resigned his post. Then followed another Council, and then another deputy governor, so that in ten years the form of government was changed no less than six times.

When William III. took the province away from Penn, he appointed a captain general, Colonel Benjamin Fletcher, who served until the colony was given back to Penn, a year and ten months later. Then Penn appointed his cousin, Markham, to be deputy governor, with two assistants. Markham, although he had a troubled time of it, managed to keep charge until William Penn was able to join him in 1699. All this time Penn had been paying salaries and spending money on his home at Pennsbury, and had been receiving nothing in return.

There was another reason for Penn's returning
to his colony as soon as he could, and that was that
King William was growing impatient at the stories
he heard of the misgovernment of Pennsylvania,
and was determined that something should be done
to put things on a more stable footing. So, under
the urging of friends at court who knew the king's
mind, Penn collected what money he could, and on
September 9, 1699, embarked with his wife and
his daughter Letitia on the ship *Canterbury* at
Southampton. The voyage was long and stormy,
but three months later — toward the end of November — the ship reached the mouth of the Delaware River. The ship was so slow in sailing up
the river that when New Castle was reached, Penn
left her and was rowed to Chester.

Many settlers, hearing of the arrival of the
proprietor of the province, flocked to Chester to
greet him. Among them was a Quaker who had
been well known in England, Thomas Story, who
had traveled extensively in America. Penn and
Story spent the night together at the house of
Lydia Wade, near Chester, and Story told the
proprietor all that had been happening in the
province, including the scourge of yellow fever, or
"Barbadoes distemper," as it was often called,
that had visited Philadelphia a short time before

and proved fatal to more than two hundred people.

Next day Penn returned to the *Canterbury* and sailed on up to Philadelphia. Here he landed, paid a short visit to Markham, the deputy governor, and then went to the Quaker meetinghouse, where he preached to a great congregation.

THE SLATE-ROOF HOUSE. (SEE PAGE 128.)

He brought with him to Philadelphia a young man named James Logan, who acted as his secretary; in time Logan became Penn's chief representative, and one of the wisest of those who helped to govern the province.

Penn had no house of his own in Philadelphia, so he, with his wife, his daughter Letitia, and James Logan, stayed for a month at the house of Edward Shippen, and then moved to one of the largest houses of the town, then known as "the slate-roof house"; it stood on the east side of Second Street between Chestnut and Walnut. There his son John was born, and the boy was always affection- ately known as "John the American."

Most of the people of Pennsylvania, and par- ticularly the Quakers, were very glad to have Penn with them again. He was a man well able to govern, but not generally successful in choosing others to govern for him. There was one man, Colonel Quarry, who had been sowing dissension and distrust of Penn in the province, but Penn sent for him, and after a talk, Quarry admitted that he had been wrong and the two became friends. One of the things Penn soon learned, a thing that seems strange enough to us, was that there was a good deal of piracy going on in the neighborhood of his province, and that many of the pirates were actually living in comfort in Phila- delphia! It did not take Penn long to get after these men, and he soon had them arrested and punished in a way that spoke well for his energy and zeal. Other crimes and wrongs he punished or corrected,. and the Quakers soon found they were right in believing that their governor was as good an executive as he was a preacher.

He was very busy that winter, holding meetings of his Council and passing new laws, preaching to Quakers in Pennsylvania and New Jersey, surveying a manor of ten thousand acres at Rockhill, in Bucks County, for his son John, and overseeing repairs to his country place at Pennsbury. Incidentally, it is interesting to recall that, liberal and freedom-loving as he was, it had not occurred to him to oppose the custom of holding negro slaves, for he himself had many slaves in his own employment.

He urged the settlers to make their prisons not merely places of restraint but workhouses and reformatories, and as a result Pennsylvania prisons were far better managed than those in other colonies. He introduced the custom of having a night watchman go through the streets, calling out the hour, the state of the weather, and any news of interest. In many ways he improved conditions, showing that he had a real genius for governing and an intense desire to make his province an ideal place in which to live.

Early in the spring of 1700 he moved to his mansion at Pennsbury, twenty miles up the river. It was built of bricks, most of which had been

ĸ.

brought from England, and it stood about one hundred rods from the bank of the Delaware.

PENN'S DESK.

Back of it were deep forests, penetrated by only a few roads and trails. It was said to have cost £5000 to build, a very large sum for a house in the wilderness, but it was the most imposing residence to be found anywhere between the Hudson and Potomac rivers, and had few equals in New York or Virginia.

The house had two stories, with a high attic for servants' rooms, and the main walls were eighteen inches thick. There was a large hall on the first floor, where Penn held meetings of his Council, gave entertainments, and welcomed the Indian chiefs who frequently came to see him. A parlor and a drawing-room were to the north of the hall, a

library and a dining-room to the south. As was
the custom then, the kitchen was a separate building, but connected with the mansion by a covered
passageway. Back of the kitchen was a building
called "the brewhouse," where ale and "strong
beer" were brewed. There was also a laundry and
a stable for twelve horses, and at either end of the
main house were small buildings, one of which was
Penn's office for the transaction of the affairs of
his province, the other for the business of his
private estate. This was the way in which the
large landowners of colonial times planned their
homes and business offices.

When Penn visited Philadelphia, he usually went
down the Delaware in his private barge, rowed by
six oarsmen. He seems to have enjoyed this mode
of travel, and to have taken great pleasure in the
scenery along the broad river. Gardens stretched
from his house to the water front, and he trans-
planted many native wild flowers to his own
grounds, besides setting out walnuts, hawthorns,
hazels, and fruit trees that he brought from England.

He lived in fine style; for William Penn, in spite
of his urging simplicity in all things, could always
appreciate and enjoy luxury. He had very handsome oak and walnut chairs and tables, satin

curtains, a wine cellar well stocked, and six large cisterns for holding water or beer. Frequently he played the part of host to many Indians, and it is said that he once entertained them at a long table spread out-of-doors, serving a hundred turkeys and a large quantity of venison.

While the provincial Assembly was in session in Philadelphia Penn was very busy directing its business, but when it adjourned, he usually turned his attention to questions concerning the Indians, whom he regarded as almost as much his own people as the white settlers. When he made his first treaty with them, he planned to call them together twice each year to renew their treaty of friendship, to adjust any matters of trade that might have arisen, and to smoke the pipe of peace with them. His absence in England had for a long time made these meetings impossible, but he now resumed them, and called the chiefs into conference with him.

The Delaware and Susquehanna tribes, who had now enjoyed his fair treatment for almost twenty years, were anxious to have Penn make agreements with other tribes, more especially those who lived in the country along the Potomac River. So they went to Onas, as Penn was usually called, and he agreed to meet their allies in April, 1701.

At this meeting there came to see him many leading Indians, — three kings, and the brother of the
Emperor of the Five Nations, as well as forty other
chiefs. With all these Penn made treaties of peace
and trade, by which the Indians were to be pro-
tected from the greed and cunning of white traders,
and were, on their part, to sell their furs and skins
only to Pennsylvanians. In this way he contrived
to keep the red men friendly to the whites in his
province, and gained the great benefit of having a
bulwark of friendly Indians to protect his colony
from enemies. When he made one of these treaties,
he sent word of it to the government in England,
and so increased his already well-deserved reputation of knowing how to deal with the Indians better
than any other governor of an English colony.

At Pennsbury the family lived much like a family
of high rank in England. The ladies dressed in silk
and wore elaborate caps and buckles and golden
ornaments. Penn himself bought no less than four
wigs in one year at a cost of nearly twenty pounds.
But if he was indulgent to his family and himself,
he was always looking after the poor and the sick.
When he heard of men or women in prison for debt,
he contrived to get them out and start them
afresh ; he was always ready to listen to and help
those who came to him in any distress, and he gave

pensions of three shillings a week to many old
people who were no longer able to support themselves. His private cash books show a long list of
generous giving that far outstrips the sums he
spent for his own household use.

Besides his barge on the river he had a coach, a
calash, and a sedan chair. He was very fond of
good horses, and had a number in his stables.
Often, however, he found it easier to explore the
neighboring country on foot than on horseback,
and he was very fond of taking long walks through
the woods. Once he was lost on a hill near Valley
Forge, and wandered about for some time when he
came to another height from which he saw the
Schuylkill River. The first hill he named Mount
Misery, and the second Mount Joy, and these
names stuck to the hills for some time.

A pleasant little incident is told of how, as William Penn was riding one day to the Quaker meetinghouse at Haverford, outside Philadelphia, he
overtook a little barefooted girl, Rebecca Wood,
who was also going to the meeting. He took her
up behind him on the horse, and the two rode on to
the meetinghouse, the little girl's bare legs making
an odd constrast to the tall governor in his long
coat and knee breeches.

William and Hannah Penn entertained continually at their country home, preferring Pennsbury to the town. Penn's daughter Letitia, however, who was twenty years old, and a very lively, handsome girl, did not care so much for the quiet of the country, and spent most of her time in Philadelphia with the Markhams, the Logans, or the Shippens.

Penn always dealt fairly with the Indians, and they trusted him far more than they did most of the white men. He traveled through New Jersey, New York, and Maryland, being eager to see the country and also to spread Quaker influence as widely as he could in the new world. The life of a country gentleman suited him to perfection, and he was undoubtedly much happier in Pennsylvania than he had been when a courtier at Whitehall in London, or striving to make other people believe that King James was as worthy a king as he himself thought him.

Still, the government of Pennsylvania did not run smoothly even while Penn was there. Quakers and Church of England people were constantly wrangling, and the Assembly would not pass the laws that Penn thought it ought to. He was not making money from his province; he still had to pay large salaries, and he was constantly being asked for money for various purposes. Once he

declared that the province had meant a loss to him
of £20,000. Occasionally he received payment
from the sale of land or for rent, but the settlers
were hard people to deal with and paid out their
money grudgingly.

The limits of Pennsylvania were still very in-
definite, and for the most part were not settled
until years later. The province was said to be
bounded on the north by the southern limits of
New York, and on the south by the northern limits
of Maryland. Neither of these boundaries was
actually settled until 1768. Westward the boundary was yet more vague, being defined by the
words "as far to the westward as Maryland ex-
tends." But boundaries were not of great impor-
tance then, when there was so much vacant land,
although by 1702 great numbers of Germans, Swiss,
Huguenots, and Scotch-Irish were coming into the
province and taking up homesteads west and north
of the little Quaker settlement on the Delaware.

The Pennsylvania Assembly refused to grant
certain supplies that were asked by King William
in 1701, and at the same time a bill was presented
in the English Parliament to change the government of the English colonies in America. By this
bill West and East Jersey were to be annexed to
New York, and Penn's charter was to be revoked,

he being paid a certain sum in return, and his province turned into a Crown colony similar to New York. When Penn heard of this, he thought that he ought to return to England and fight it. This he expected would take him only a short time, and he planned to return to Pennsbury at the end of a year. He wanted to make his home there, and expected his wife and Letitia to stay there until he returned. But his family thought otherwise about being left behind. Penn wrote to James Logan: "I can not prevail on my wife to stay: still less Tishe. I know not what to do." And in another letter he wrote: "The going of my wife and Tishe will add greatly to the expense; more of living in London than of the passage. But they will not be denied."

Both Mrs. Penn and Letitia were probably homesick for their native England. Letitia in particular missed her gay friends at home, and found the Quakers of the province a poor substitute. It happened that later, when she did return to England, she gave up the Quaker faith and became a member of the Church of England. Mrs. Penn, in addition to other reasons for returning home, had already seen that her husband required the help of her firm will and clear insight when he was beset with political troubles in England, and believed she could be of great assistance to him. So when Penn did return, he took his family with him.

He made Andrew Hamilton deputy governor of the province, and James Logan secretary; and on November 4, 1701, sailed from Philadelphia in the ship *Dalmahoy*. The ship made a very quick run, in fact one of the fastest voyages recorded at that time, taking only thirty-six days to cross; and by the middle of December Penn was again in London. He took apartments in Kensington, that he might be close to the king and Parliament in looking after his title to his province.

It turned out that Penn never went back to Pennsylvania again, although some of his children did. Politics were to take all his attention; he was to have no more of the country life in America that he had grown so fond of, and that seemed to bring out all the best qualities in his many-sided nature.

CHAPTER XIII

At Court and in Prison

WILLIAM PENN still had many friends at court, and it was doubtless largely through their efforts that he succeeded in having the bill to take Pennsylvania away from him withdrawn from Parliament. There were a number of prominent men in the government, however, who thought that none of the American colonies should be owned by private persons, but that all should be directly under the Crown, and these men soon offered another bill much like the earlier one. To defeat this, Penn and Lord Baltimore joined hands and ceased to wrangle over the boundary between Pennsylvania and Maryland. A few days after this bill was presented in Parliament, however, King William died from injuries resulting from the fall of a horse he was riding. The king had been influential in urging the change in the government of Penn's province, but his successor, Queen Anne, was much more friendly to Penn. The matter was therefore allowed to drop.

Although the daughter of James Stuart, Queen Anne was a Protestant, and had married a Protestant, Prince George of Denmark. She was liberal to all religions, and soon after she became queen the Quakers asked Penn to present her with an address thanking her for the toleration toward all sects that she had promised to observe. Penn read the address. Queen Anne then answered graciously enough, "Mr. Penn, I am so well pleased that what I have said is to your satisfaction, that you and your friends may be assured of my protection, and I sincerely hope for your welfare and happiness."

She kept her word to the Quakers, and also proved the constant friend of Penn. She had seen him much at court when her father was king, and knew of the old friendship between her father and the Quaker leader. Therefore Penn became in a way a courtier again, and held somewhat the same prominent position he had held before William came to the throne.

He spent much of his time in London, where he now had friends in both the Whig and Tory parties. The leading statesmen thought so highly of his abilities that they frequently asked him to arrange political and personal matters that required tact and diplomatic skill. Sometimes he tried to exer-

cise these qualities by correspondence with the law-
makers of Pennsylvania, and one of his latest efforts
was on behalf of the negro slaves in the province.
Ten years before he had tried to get justice done
to these people, but in vain. Now he felt more
strongly than ever that it was wrong to import
negroes into the new country as slaves. He worked
for this object until he induced the colonial Assembly to try to discourage that traffic by placing a
duty on the importing of slaves. In 1711 they
prohibited such importation in the future, but no
sooner had word of this good law reached England
than the government there, in spite of Penn's
efforts, canceled the Pennsylvania act. Yet the
wisest statesmen in England realized that Penn
was right, and that the course he was urging his
colony to adopt, not only in regard to negro slavery
but in all matters that dealt with human liberty and
enlightenment, was the best for the new world to
follow.

Of Penn's children by his first wife, the lively
Letitia married William Aubrey, who was harsh
and overbearing to her father and tyrannical toward her. His son William had married, but had
become very dissipated during his father's visit to
Pennsylvania, and was now the black sheep of the
family. He owed a great many debts and was in

danger of being put into prison for them, so Penn decided he would be better off in Pennsylvania, and sent him out to Pennsbury. He was to be encouraged to live a healthy outdoor life, and have horses and hounds for hunting foxes, deer, and wolves. The son went out to Pennsbury, and James Logan tried to keep a watchful and restraining eye on him, but he managed to get into almost as much trouble there as he had in London, in spite of all efforts to keep him straight.

A great change had come over England since the days when the Stuarts were sovereigns. The old brutal laws had been abolished for the most part, and there was far less cruelty and violence. Instead of the dissolute Charles and the treacherous James, the rulers were honorable and virtuous. There were no longer constant rumors of plots and conspiracies, and all religions were treated fairly. William Penn found that he was no longer needed to help some poor Quaker who had fallen under the disfavor of officers of the law. Now his difficulties were mainly those connected with trying to provide a decent government for his province, and to get enough money from it to pay expenses.

Before Penn left Pennsylvania the Assembly there had voted to pay him £2000, but that was soon spent, and the settlers were so economical that

they did not wish to give him anything more.
Again and again he wrote to James Logan about
his financial difficulties in managing Pennsylvania.
In one letter he said: "Never had poor man my
task, with neither men nor money to assist me. I
therefore strictly charge thee that thou represent
to Friends there, that I am forced to borrow money,
and add debts to debts, instead of paying them off.
. . . Make return with all speed or I'm undone."

He tried many ways to make his province pay
him something in return for the work and money he
had already bestowed on it. He urged Logan to buy
and send him as many furs as he could get, knowing
that they would bring a good price in England.
At one time he thought of selling his government
directly to the English Crown for a sum sufficient
to pay off all his debts. There was considerable
haggling about the price and the sale was never
made. Meantime his son William was getting
into more trouble at Pennsbury and in Philadelphia. One night he and a dissipated comrade
began to beat the night watch. He received a
thrashing, and was afterwards treated as a common
rioter. The son had been given a manor in the
hope that he would look after it, but instead he
sold it and squandered all the money. At last
Penn sent for him to come home, and when William

the younger finally reached England, he took to his former way of living, and incurred fresh debts for his already impoverished and indulgent parent.

Penn figured that he had lost £30,000 by his province. "O Pennsylvania," he wrote, "what hast thou cost me! Above £30,000 more than I ever got by it, two hazardous and most fatiguing voyages, my straits and slavery here, and my child's soul almost. . . . In short, I must sell all or be undone, and disgraced into the bargain."

The man who was now acting as deputy governor of Pennsylvania was proving a poor makeshift, and conditions in the province seemed to be going from bad to worse. Opposition to Penn himself also was increasing, and presently the Assembly passed a set of resolutions that were sent to him in London. These resolutions made many complaints against his government of the province, charging him with having sided with enemies of the colony, with having extorted money from settlers in the sale of lands, with having failed to pay a former governor's salary, and ended by stating that something must be done to suppress lawlessness in the province. When it became known that the Assembly had sent such a note to Penn, the colonists at once objected to the offensiveness of its tone. Orders were given to recall the resolutions, and, in an attempt to straighten the matter out, the Assembly voted £1200 for the support of Penn's government. All might now have gone smoothly had not the deputy governor, John Evans, tried to scare the Quakers by a foolish trick. He had been wanting to build up a militia for the province, but the Quakers had objected to this. So, on the day of the annual fair, Evans arranged to have a messenger ride into Philadelphia, bringing the exciting news that a force of French soldiers had been seen on the Delaware heading toward Philadelphia. Then Evans buckled on his sword and rode up and down before the people, urging them to arm and defend their province.

There was a brief alarm, during which the larger ships on the Delaware were hurried up the river while the smaller craft were concealed in creeks. Silverware and valuables were hidden, but only four men came to the meeting-place Evans had appointed to enroll as militiamen. When it was discovered how Evans had tried to trick them, the settlers were highly indignant, and sent a complaint to Penn in England. Penn also heard that there was much criticism of his friend and secretary, James Logan.

A few of the men in whom Penn trusted, like James Logan, were entirely worthy of his trust,

L

but there were many who were not. Among these
latter was a man named Philip Ford, a Quaker,
who had for some time been acting as steward of
Penn's estates in England and Ireland. Penn
grew very fond of Ford, as he had been very fond
of James Stuart, and at length made him a present
of ten thousand acres in Pennsylvania, a city lot
in Philadelphia, and one hundred and fifty acres
in the suburbs.

Ford sent accounts to Penn from time to time,
but Penn was not a good business man, and did
not bother to look into the accounts. Finally,
when he did, he found the surprising fact that although Ford had received from Penn £17,000 and
had only spent £16,000, nevertheless Penn owed
him £10,500. Ford brought about this result by
charging very large commissions, adding compound
interest every six months to all money advanced,
and claiming an exceedingly large salary, to say
nothing of sometimes failing to credit Penn with
money actually received from him.

Yet Penn, although surprised at this new debt,
made no investigation into the crooked accounts,
and at length, when Ford kept urging him to pay
the debt, Penn was so foolish as to give Ford a
deed of the province of Pennsylvania as security
for this claim that he did not really owe. To make

matters worse, a little later Penn accepted from Ford a lease of the province, so that it appeared that he had actually transferred the province to this corrupt steward and was now leasing it from him.

None of this strange transaction was made public until Ford died, but then his widow and son declared how the matter stood and announced that they were the legal owners of Pennsylvania. Penn, they said, was merely their tenant, and they sued him for rent amounting to £3000. They got judgment against him, and then, when he failed to pay it, had him arrested and put in prison for the debt. So now we find the owner of the great province of Pennsylvania not only shorn of his title to his property, but actually in jail on a charge of failing to pay his rent.

When the officers came to arrest him, they found him at the Quaker meeting in Gracechurch Street in London, strange to say the very place where he had first been arrested thirty-seven years before for preaching to the Quakers.

For nine months Penn had to stay in prison, while the suit against him dragged slowly through the courts of chancery. The fact that he had paid so little attention to Ford's accounts, and had made no complaint about the figures in them, made it look as if the claim against him might be just. His friends tried to straighten out the tangled matter, and meantime Penn, who was allowed fairly comfortable quarters, held small religious meetings, and kept himself as serene and untroubled as in the heyday of his fortunes. In this again the strong character of William Penn appears, for he was not cast down by misfortune. His friend Isaac Norris bore witness to this quality. "After all," said Norris, "I think the fable of the palm good in him — 'the more he is pressed, the more he rises.' He seems a spirit fit to bear and rub through difficulties, and as thou observes his foundation remains. I have been at some meetings with him, and have been much comforted in them, and particularly last First-day."

Gradually public sympathy, especially among the Quakers, began to be aroused by the fact of Penn's imprisonment. He had done so much for the Quaker cause, and had tried so hard to give his province a good government, that people were indignant that he should now be so set upon by such people as the Fords. So friends raised the sum of £7600, and gave this to the Fords in settlement of their claim, and in return Penn gave his friends a mortgage on Pennsylvania to secure the repayment of the money they had lent him.

Meantime, while he was still in prison, his deputy governor Evans had been behaving so badly that the people of the province decided they would stand him no longer. Penn, having once felt a strong friendship for this man, would have put up with almost any injustice from him. Three prominent Quakers went to him in the Fleet Prison, however, and told him that unless he removed Evans from the governorship the people would appeal to Queen Anne to settle the matter. This might result in taking the province from him; so, reluctantly, Penn agreed to dismiss Evans from his position. Even then, however, he was so fond of Evans that he would not let him know that he disapproved of his acts. He wrote to James Logan, asking him to explain the matter to his deputy governor, and said, "Pray break it to him and that the reason why I chose to change, rather than contest with the complaints before the queen in council, is, that he may stand the fairer for any employment elsewhere; which would be very doubtful if those blemishes were aggravated in such a presence."

In place of Evans, Penn sent out as the new governor another friend of his, Colonel Charles Gookin. He wrote very flattering accounts of this new governor to the people of Philadelphia.

Stanchness in standing by his friends, even when

it was shown that those friends were utterly untrust-
worthy, had proved nearly as disastrous to William
Penn in the government of his province as it had
proved to his fortunes in England in the days when
he had supported James Stuart against King William.   It may have been a fine fault, but a fault it
was, nevertheless.

CHAPTER XIV

WHEN Penn left the Fleet Prison, he went to his home at Brentford, nine miles out of London, and stayed there for a short time, after which he moved with his family to a country place in the Berkshire Hills called Ruscombe. While he was here he kept up his efforts to sell Pennsylvania to the English Crown, and, as that matter dragged along with little result, he tried his best to straighten out the tangled government of his colony by sending long letters to James Logan and other officers in Philadelphia. In its early days the province had been a great pleasure to him, but now it seemed to be only a source of continual misunderstandings and debts. He felt that, however much the colony might have profited others, it had proved almost a thankless burden to himself. He wrote to some of the colonists just what his feelings were in regard to Pennsylvania. "The many combats I have engaged in," he said, "the great pains and incredible expense to your welfare and ease, to the decay of my former estate, of which (however some there would represent it) I too sensibly feel the effects, with the undeserved opposition I have met with from thence, sink me into sorrow, that if not supported by a superior hand, might have overwhelmed me long ago. And I cannot but think it hard measure, that, while that has proved a land of freedom and flourishing, it should become to me, by whose means it was principally made a country, the cause of grief, trouble, and poverty."

Although the English Crown was anxious to take over the province of Pennsylvania, there were many obstacles to their coming to an agreement with Penn. Some of these obstacles he at length compromised; for example, he agreed that he and his family should have only 800,000 acres in fee, in place of all the rights to real estate that had been granted him under the original charter. He insisted that there should be no official establishing of the Church of England in Pennsylvania, that no public money should be used for one sect in preference to others, and that public offices should be open to all settlers. After much controversy the English government drew up a new charter or constitution, modeled after those in New York and New Jersey, except that nothing whatever was said in the charter about establishing the Church

of England; while the question of the right to vote
on public matters was left for the people themselves
to decide.

By 1710 the arrangements to take over Pennsylvania from Penn were about completed. He then
wrote a long letter to the people of his province,
addressing them as "My Old Friends," and setting
forth what he had tried to do for them, and how
of late they had pained him by their continual
squabbles. His writing showed his surprise that
Pennsylvania had not been the home of peace he
expected it would be. In one part of the letter he
said, "Friends! the eyes of many are upon you;
the people of many nations of Europe look on that
country as a land of ease and quiet, wishing to
themselves in vain the same blessings they con-
ceive you may enjoy; but to see the use you make
of them is no less the cause of surprise to others,
while such bitter complaints and reflections are
seen to come from you, of which it is difficult to con-
ceive either the sense or meaning. What are the
distresses, grievances, and oppressions, that the
papers, sent from thence, so often say you lan-
guish under, while others have cause to believe
you have hitherto lived, or might live, the happiest
of any in the Queen's dominions?" He graciously
closed his letter in these words: "God give you

his wisdom and fear to direct you, that yet our
poor country may be blessed with peace, love, and
industry, and we may once more meet good friends,
and live so to the end, our relation in the Truth
having but the same true interest. I am, with
great truth and most sincere regard, your real
friend, as well as just Proprietor and Governor,
William Penn."

The English Crown was to pay Penn £12,000 in
four annual installments. Before the matter could
be finally settled it had to be ratified by an Act of
Parliament; however, there seemed little reason to
doubt but that the affair was practically settled,
and so Penn considered it. Although he was
now almost seventy years old, he made many
journeys through England in order to spread the
Quaker doctrines. In his leisure moments he
added many maxims to the collection he had made,
and did other writing as well. He seems to have
given up the idea of returning to his house at
Pennsbury, although he sometimes spoke as if he
should like to return, if only his affairs in London
would let him do so.

Some time before he had been taken ill, having
what appeared to be a stroke of paralysis. He
recovered from this, but a second recurrence of
his illness came, and then a third. This last made

him a complete invalid, and even affected his mind
to a certain degree. Although calm and serene, he
could not transact business intelligently. This
prevented the completion of the sale of his title to
Pennsylvania; for, his mind being impaired, he
could not give a valid deed to the government. As
a result the title to the province stayed in his family
until the American Revolution in 1776.

When he could not attend to matters in Pennsylvania, his wife took charge, and she managed them
very capably. It was she who discharged a deputy
governor who was quarreling with the Assembly
there, and appointed in his place an excellent governor, Sir William Keith, who proved a popular and
very successful officer. Also, trade in Pennsylvania
was now beginning to boom, so that in a short time
the province became much more valuable, and it
turned out well for Penn's wife and children that
he had not sold his title to the English Crown.

Penn remained an invalid until his death on
July 30, 1718, and during this time, freed from care
concerning his province, he delighted in the quiet
country life at Ruscombe, and in the company of
his devoted wife and younger children. Many
friends came to visit him, and on Sundays he was
driven to the meetinghouse, where he would sometimes speak briefly, always proclaiming his faith in

the religion that had been the guide and mainstay of his eventful life.

William Penn was always a deeply religious and honorable man, thoroughly sincere, and indomitable in his defense of what he believed to be the truth. He was a great man, for he led the new sect of Quakers through their early trials; he had the vision to build them a new home beyond the seas and to set them standards of liberty and government that were far in advance of his time. His faults of judgment were many; he too often trusted the wrong men, and frequently he showed himself a child in caring for money matters. These faults, however, were never faults of character, but rather of a nature too generous and confiding. We usually think of him as a quiet, simple Quaker, wearing plain clothes and caring little or nothing for luxury or display. In reality he was quite different. He was a man of action, a man who was naturally fond of court life, who liked power, who was restless and eager, and who would have made a better soldier than a statesman. While he lived in Pennsylvania he lived up to his idea of a great landed proprietor and governor, and he liked to be regarded as the leading man among the Quakers both in Pennsylvania and in England.

His province of Pennsylvania was at once the

TABLET TO THE MEMORY OF WILLIAM PENN.

This beautiful tablet was erected and dedicated by the Pennsylvania Society, in the Church of All Hallows, London, on July 13, 1911.

delight and the torment of his existence. He liked his ideal of what such a colony ought to be, but he found the actual management of it one long series of quarrels and money difficulties. He dealt fairly with settlers and Indians, probably more fairly than any other governor of an American colony, and the Indians seemed to appreciate his fair dealing more than did the white men. The colony owed something to his guidance, but a great deal more to the noble spirit of liberty of religion in which he founded it. There is to be found what has made the name of William Penn illustrious and beloved, for he had a great vision of human liberty and he worked mightily to make that vision become a reality. In the light of his splendid ambitions his mistakes count for little. He tried to do great good, which is the best that can be said of any man.

CHAPTER XV

WILLIAM PENN'S son by his first wife, named for himself, the one who had been sent to Pennsylvania in the hope that he would give over his wild way of living, inherited the property in England and Ireland, most of which had belonged to his mother. Letitia, who had married William Aubrey, had already received a dower, and later received ten thousand acres of land in Pennsylvania, as did each of the younger William's children, Gulielma, Maria, Springett, and William. The remainder of Penn's estate went to his second wife, Hannah Penn, and her five children, John, Thomas, Margaret, Richard, and Dennis. Hannah Penn had practically all the powers over the province that her husband had wielded, and she used them capably, proving a most excellent business woman. She arranged that her eldest son, John, should become the principal Proprietary of the province, as he was called, and his brothers Thomas and Richard his associates. The youngest son, Dennis, died very young.

From 1712 to 1727 Hannah Penn managed the affairs of Pennsylvania, and far more successfully than her husband had done. He had left his province in such a debt-ridden condition that it had seemed as if it would have to be sold to the Crown to straighten it out, but Hannah Penn left it to her three sons in such excellent shape that it was generally considered to be one of the finest domains in the world owned by private individuals.

Sir William Keith, the governor who had been appointed by Hannah Penn, managed affairs with success for some time, but finally came disagreements with Mrs. Penn. He believed that her son John would not make a good manager of the province, and secretly advised the popular leaders in the colony to try to abolish the Proprietary system of government. This caused Hannah Penn to appoint Patrick Gordon to succeed Governor Keith in 1726.

In 1732 Thomas Penn made a visit to Pennsylvania, and he was followed by his older brother John in 1734. Neither of these sons of William Penn made a good impression in Philadelphia, and it is said that the people there even preferred young William Penn, with all his bad manners and wildness, to these two half-brothers of his. Neither John nor Thomas seem to have had the broadmindedness and kindly disposition of their father, but to have been unscrupulous, overbearing, and too eager to make all the money they could out of the colony. John was somewhat better liked than Thomas, who seemed to have little sense about anything but money-getting. Benjamin Franklin, who was editor of the *Pennsylvania Gazette* during the visit of the two sons of Penn to Philadelphia, but who had never met the roystering young William, is reported to have said to a friend that "according to all accounts there was more of the gentleman in Billy Penn drunk than in both of these Penns sober."

John Penn returned to England in 1736, and Thomas in 1741, and neither ever returned to Pennsylvania, having about as much affection for their father's province as the province had for them.

Governor Gordon, who had been appointed by Hannah Penn, had a successful administration and held the office until his death in 1736. The Penn brothers then chose George Thomas to the place, and he proved a most loyal adherent of England until he resigned in 1747. James Hamilton, the first governor of Pennsylvania who was born and bred in America, succeeded him, and proved the most popular governor since William Penn had made his second visit to his province. Governor Hamilton felt that Pennsylvania would be better off as an English colony than under the proprietorship of the Penn family, and most of the people agreed with him, but no definite steps in that direction were taken. John Penn had died, and the two brothers who survived him, Thomas and Richard, knew that Hamilton was too popular with the Pennsylvanians to be removed from office. After a while, however, disagreements developed to such a degree that Hamilton resigned, and the governors who followed had to face new difficulties arising from the fact that the French were influencing the Indians against the English colonists, in Pennsylvania no less than in New England and New York. William Penn's policy of fair dealing with the Indians had been abandoned by his sons, and the frontiersmen were made to feel the result in constant attacks on their outlying settlements.

The Quakers did not believe in warfare, but the men on the Pennsylvania frontiers, Scotch-Irish, Swiss, and Germans, had to arm and form companies for self-protection after General Braddock's defeat by the French and Indians. They felt that they ought to have some help, financial if no other, from the wealthy people in the eastern part of the

M

province; and at length they succeeded in getting the Assembly to vote for supplies. When it came to raising this money, the property of the Penns had to be taxed, and this gave the greatest offense to Thomas and Richard Penn in England. They removed the governor, and tried to fight the tax, but the colonists replied by voting the tax again and even increasing the amount the Penns had to pay. The governor who had been removed told Franklin that he was glad to be rid of the job, adding that three years of the governorship as he had held it would turn any man against the Proprietary system. To which Franklin answered, "Particularly with Tom and Dick Penn for Proprietors !"

In 1763 John Penn, the son of Richard, and grandson of William Penn, became governor, and his term of office was the stormiest and least creditable of all the governorships that the province had known. During his first year in office a revolt took place in the mountains which became known as the "revolution of the Paxton boys." A crowd of mountaineers defied a battalion of British regulars in the town of Lancaster, and announced that if the regulars dared to fire "so much as one shot, their scalps would ornament every cabin from the Susquehanna to the Ohio."

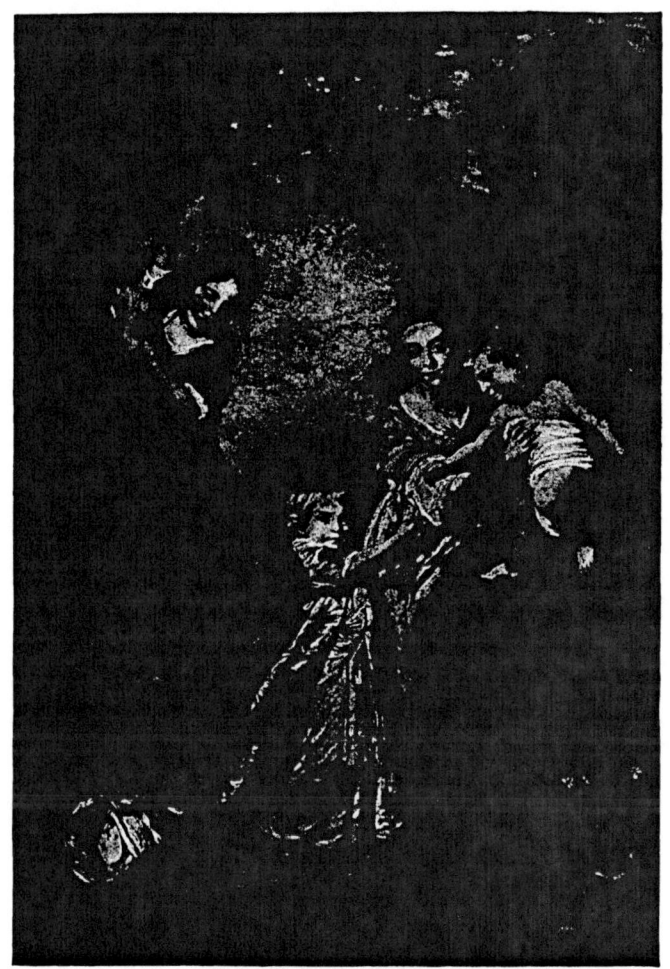

From " The Family of William Penn," by Howard M. Jenkins.

FOUR OF WILLIAM PENN'S GRANDCHILDREN.

Painted by Sir Joshua Reynolds.

The picture shows the children of Thomas Penn — Juliana, Louisa Hannah,
John, and Granville.

The soldiers did not fire, and the Paxton boys thereupon helped themselves to all the horses they wanted, took the ammunition wagons belonging to the regulars, and set out for Philadelphia. There were almost a thousand of them when they arrived on the high ground of Germantown, and there demanded that certain Indians who were being kept under guard in the Northern Liberties [1] should be given to them on pain of their sacking the city otherwise.

The citizens found that the regular troops could not be relied on, and sent some deputies to treat with the rebels. By agreeing to all the latter demanded, except the massacre of the Indians, the deputies were finally able to induce the mountaineers to return to their homes.

Very soon afterward the Assembly petitioned the English Parliament to abolish the Proprietary

[1] It is interesting to recall that this term, "Liberties," had been applied to certain tracts of land lying north and west of the original limits of Philadelphia. The soil contained in these tracts was called "liberty land" or "free lots" because William Penn had made a gift of land in these sections to the first purchasers of lots in the city proper, the amount of "free" land given being in proportion to the amount of "town" land that was bought. The term, "City and Liberties of Philadelphia," was commonly used in the early days of the province, the city containing about 1820 acres, and the Liberties about 16,236 acres. Later, the Northern Liberties became a part of the city of Philadelphia.

government. Before Parliament did this, however, another misadventure had occurred in the province. About 1762 fifty families from Connecticut had moved to the Wyoming Valley of Pennsylvania, and believing the country there to be very productive, they had made some clearings, built log cabins, and grown some fields of corn. John Penn, the governor, heard of this, and in 1764 he sent constables to this settlement to order the pioneers off, claiming that they were on land that had been granted to his grandfather.

The Wyoming settlement now numbered about three thousand persons, and naturally they were unwilling to give up their lands. Then a company was formed in Philadelphia to buy that section of the country from John Penn, and, making use of the improvements of the Connecticut settlers, market it as the company saw fit. They would only buy it, however, on condition that John Penn should first drive out the settlers.

So John Penn, in 1770, hired a crowd of rascals to go into the Wyoming Valley and drive the pioneers away from their cabins and fields. The settlers answered Penn's demands by building a fort which they christened Forty Fort, in honor of the first settlers, who were forty in number. They were always referred to as the First Forty, and were held in high esteem. They had been sent by the Susquehanna Company of Connecticut into the Wyoming Valley.

After some fighting the settlers managed to hold their ground. This became known as the Pennamite War; and, although the governor was backed by some of the leading men of Philadelphia, his attempts to oust the settlers made his rule more distasteful than ever to a people who were growing more and more fond of liberty.

The American Revolution was now at hand, and the Pennsylvania Committee of Safety decided that it was time to annul the charter that had been granted to William Penn, and abolish the Proprietary government. Therefore, two months after the Declaration of Independence was signed, in 1776, the Committee of Safety, now calling itself the "Supreme Executive Council," deposed John Penn from his office, and decreed that what had been the province of Pennsylvania should become a state in the new American Union.

The boundaries of Pennsylvania were by that time definitely settled, and incidentally those boundaries included the rich Wyoming Valley, where now stands the prosperous city of Wilkes-Barre. The title that had belonged to the Penn family was now vested in the state, and the state appropriated £130,000 to be paid to the heirs of William Penn. In addition to this amount the heirs of William Penn, having sided with the Tories during the Revolution, claimed a large sum from the English government after the Revolution, basing their claim on the Act of Parliament that agreed "to indemnify loyal subjects of his Britannic Majesty for losses suffered in the American War." The English government settled this claim by paying William Penn's heirs £500,000. As a result these heirs secured from Pennsylvania and from England more than three million dollars, besides retaining the private estates in Pennsylvania that they had always owned.

Eventually, therefore, Penn's province proved of very great value to his children and grandchildren, although the people who had opened up and settled that new country had gained little from those descendants; they had to look back to the great founder, William Penn, the noble and steadfast Quaker, for the liberty-loving ideas and wise principles of government that helped to make Pennsylvania one of the greatest of the new union of states. It is well that his name should forever be associated with that state, for it is the name of a man of noble character and a fearless champion of liberty.

Printed in the United States of America.

True Stories of Great Americans

Each volume illustrated, cloth, 12mo, 50 cents

It is the purpose of this new series to tell simply and attractively the life stories of Americans who have achieved greatness in different fields of endeavor. The author has been chosen in each instance either because he is particularly interested in the subject of the biography or is connected with him by blood-ties and possessed, therefore, of valuable facts. Only those, however, who have shown that they have an appreciation of what makes really good juvenile literature have been intrusted with a volume. The result is that the books are graphic, vivid reviews of the principal events in the careers of these makers of the nation.

THE MACMILLAN COMPANY
Publishers   64–66 Fifth Avenue   New York

The Kingdom of the Winding Road

By CORNELIA MEIGS

With illustrations in color and in black and white by FRANCES WHITE

Cloth, 12mo

A fanciful story relating the experiences of a beggar as he travels the country over in his tattered red cloak and playing his penny flute — in reality a wonderful magical pipe. He always knows the best thing to be done and he comes to the aid of the hero when he is in the worst distress. In his own fashion he helps the bad and the good alike. The book is part fairy tale, part romance, part allegory, but always literature. In a very human way the beggar stands for the soundness and sweetness of life and there are lessons that may be drawn from his adventures. But whether one bothers with the moral and the metaphors or not, there is an inescapable charm to the narrative and an interest and appeal that increases the further one goes on the beggar's highway.

A Maid of '76

By ALDEN A. KNIPE AND EMILIE B. KNIPE

With illustrations by MRS. KNIPE

Decorated cloth, 12mo

The little heroine of this book is a girl of Revolutionary times, a patriot through and through, but whose family is loyal to the king. Out of the difficulties with which she finds herself confronted and which she brings ultimately to a satisfactory conclusion the authors have made a most entertaining story.

THE MACMILLAN COMPANY

Publishers   64-66 Fifth Avenue   New York

MACMILLAN'S JUVENILE LIBRARY

Each volume, cloth, 12mo, $.50

NEW VOLUMES

The Fairy Queen and Her Knights
By ALFRED J. CHURCH

Peggy Stewart at School
By GABRIELLE E. JACKSON

The Little King
By CHARLES MAJOR

The Voyage of the Hoppergrass
By EDMUND LESTER PEARSON

Hero Tales of the Far North
By JACOB RIIS

Gray Lady and the Birds
By MABEL OSGOOD WRIGHT

Tommy-Anne and the Three Hearts
By MABEL OSGOOD WRIGHT

Southern Soldier Stories
By GEORGE CARY EGGLESTON

The addition of these eight titles to the Juvenile Library increases the usefulness and broadens the scope of that popular series of books for younger readers. Each of these stories will be found good reading, reading of the kind which specialists in the study of child literature can heartily recommend.

THE MACMILLAN COMPANY
Publishers   64-66 Fifth Avenue   New York

The Everychild's Series

EDITED BY DR. JAMES H. VAN SICKLE

Each volume, cloth, 12mo, illustrated, 40 cents

The Everychild's Series is a library of fiction and dramatics, science and information, literature and art for children. Its contents include a wide range of subject matter, which will broaden the child's interest in plays and games, fairy-tales and fables, nature study and geography, useful arts and industries, biography and history, government and public service, myths and folk-lore, fine arts and literature.

This series seeks not only to instruct the child with simplicity, charm, and wholesomeness, but to heighten his finer appreciation of the beautiful, and to give him, along with keen enjoyment, the things of life that are interesting and valuable.

The authors of the books of this series have been chosen for their special fitness to write books for children. To each author has been given the choice of topic and method of treatment. The result is that the books in the series are not only charming and enjoyable but intellectually satisfying to the child.

The volumes are interesting and attractive in appearance. They are neatly and strongly bound in cloth with design in two colors. The type page is set leaded in large type with a wide margin. The illustrations are numerous and attractive and designed especially to represent the characters that appear in the story.

The series is a splendid source of supplementary reading material. It consists of over a score of volumes.

THE MACMILLAN COMPANY

Publishers   **64-66 Fifth Avenue**   **New York**

CPSIA information can be obtained at www.ICGtesting.com
Printed in the USA
LVOW12*2022271213

367106LV00006B/474/P